JAN —
I HOPE THAT MY "PORCHES"
WILL BRING YOU SOME FOND
MEMORIES OF YOUR OWN —
ANGELO

Porch Passages

by

Angelo Daluisio

"Porch Passages"
Angelo Daluisio
1st Edition; 2004
All photos property of Author
Ink rendering on back-cover and page 4
Courtesy of Eugene C. McHugh
Copyright; 2004
All Rights Reserved

Edited by Brad Lockwood
Kookalook Publishing
Brooklyn   Buffalo
ISBN 0-9706323-2-0

This book is dedicated to my wife Pam,
and our daughters, Danielle and Micole

Special Thanks To
Dad, Kenny, Janie, Uncle John, Wayne, and Pop.
For the countless hours unselfishly spent
with hammers, saws, wrecking bars,
brushes and rollers in-hand...
And to you, Mom and Aunt Mary,
for always finding the time to feed the troops
Italian sausage, pasta and garlic bread.

Foreword

The front porch is an American altar.

Derived from the Latin word porticus, or the Greek portico, a porch was originally a columnar entry to a classical temple. The Middle Ages brought about the use of the word in reference to a cathedral's vestibule, while Victorian times gave the connotation multiple distinctions such as veranda, piazza, loggia, and again, portico: each individual constructs in unique locations, but interchangeable as places for the public to gather. Usually covered and partially enclosed, to the front or rear of a holy structure or other prominent locale, porches, in their varying forms and assorted uses, were permanent parts of multiple cultures speaking all languages. Mostly due to climate, porches were rarely found in northern Europe, while in West Africa they were commonplace, offering shade and comfort, spiting a blistering sun. Only later though, in America, did the porch become what we now know.

More of a living area than singular entrance, attached to the frame of a house, normally the front, the great American porch came into being. What once were selective structures have been adapted to better serve the American persona. By the early 1700s, porches were spreading across the continent with pioneers, becoming an essential element of our architecture - our shared experience - by the beginning of the 1800s. Through wars and strife, conflict and community, America gathered on their porches, talking, laughing, debating, communing... As diverse as their builders, porches remain standard yet varied – wood or stone, large or small – and continue to evolve with our country.

Wide, welcoming front porches were abandoned as Americans migrated to the cities during the Industrial Revolution; relegated to tighter urban quarters, they built smaller side porches that faced their neighbors and driveways. Later – and continuing to today - as Americans migrate once more, but in reverse, from the cities to the suburbs, their new ornate homes seldom include a porch at all. Interiors air-conditioned, exteriors equipped with showy front facades and fences to the sides, porches have given way to decks. A deck is not a porch; it is not normally attached to a house, an uncovered add-on in the rear most usually; decks hardly offer the shelter of a porch. Hidden inside and behind their homes, Americans, neighbors all, now commune in lesser numbers, and are only exposed for brief moments as they open their garage doors to escape in their cars and SUVs.

Has the mighty American extroversion, interest in all things new, become subdued? Are we more solitary now, favoring the pseudo tranquility of a quarter-acre backyard over innumerable home fronts? Has our friendliness been lost, the great American adventure replaced by insecure seclusion? Or, are we all waiting for someone, anyone, brave enough to reveal their true selves? If one, just one, neighbor were to build a front porch, a structure wide and welcoming, would any follow? A fad as ancient as ourselves, no fences for cover, only each other to admire... Couldn't we all share in the joy of kinship once more?

I met Angelo Daluisio in early 2003 while hosting a writing workshop for the Just Buffalo Literary Center in Buffalo, New York. Living along the aged borders of the city, I enjoyed my home in Buffalo, but I had no front porch, only an enclosed sunroom: unfit for a gathering of any size. Angelo had a porch, though, and he wanted to write a book about it. So, while others at that workshop spoke of fighting through their first novel, or finally sharing one of the many they had already written but never let anyone else read, Angelo only wanted to talk about porches.

It seemed queer at first, truly bizarre, but he was determined to write that book; in fact, he's been writing it for the past twenty years. Started while gutting his first home and *"freeing the soul"* of the porch by tearing-out its sunroom, then rebuilding an exact replica of the original front porch that once blessed his next home in Lancaster, Angelo has been taking notes, jotting vignettes, capturing the joys of porch sitting for decades. He was almost done, he thought, and I wished him, and the others at the workshop, only the best.

I received an email one-year later. By then I had left Buffalo, moving to Brooklyn, again no front porch: there are only stoops in New York City, hard concrete steps and slabs to sit, maybe four feet wide with a cast iron barrier to rest my feet upon. Angelo's book about porches was almost done.

Almost done again?

"Let me read it." I wrote back, *"I could use a good porch right about now..."*

- Brad Lockwood
Editor & Publisher

Porch Passages

Angelo Daluisio

"Sitting here, watching the traffic go by,

kids riding their bikes down to the town pool

and squirrels running across the telephone wires.

There can't be a better way to watch the world go by

than sitting on a wonderful old porch."

*Artist's Rendering of Author's home circa early 1900s
presented to he and his wife by a neighbor, Bess McHugh.
Courtesy of Eugene C. McHugh.*

My doorbell rang today. Answering it, I saw a man standing on our front porch, a total stranger eager to ask me a few questions. Either a salesman or pollster, I didn't know, so I waited for him to introduce himself. He said that he worked at the nearby utility company. *Great! Another meter reading and more bills!* I thought... But it was nothing of the sort.

A bit abashed, he explained that he was being transferred to Binghamton, and he and his wife were having a house built in their new hometown. Perplexed, I listened, digested, then looked. In his hands were a camera and tape measure. And then it dawned on me. He wanted to take pictures and measurements of our porch. He wanted to show them to his builder and have our porch in Lancaster, New York duplicated on his new home in Binghamton, New York, some 250 miles away. Was it okay with me? Would I let him do that?

"Go right ahead." I said. Helping him, holding one end of his tape measure and offering insights: which concrete was best to use for the posts and suppliers for the spindles and railings, etc.

However unusual, this inquiry from a complete stranger wasn't the first, and certainly won't be the last. I have lost count of the number of times we have fielded questions and compliments about our porch. While building it, a carpenter friend told me that if you do something beautiful, truly special, others will take notice of it. He was right.

I owe it all to Pam, though.

My wife grew-up just up the street from this house, our home for almost twenty years now. She made me promise long ago, before we even bought it, that if we went to the VA auction and won the deed, I was to rebuild the porch the way it was when she was little. To its original splendor, no less... We were successful at the auction and got the house, but it had no porch whatsoever, only Pam's memories of what once graced the front of 53 Erie Street. The porch that Pam recalled was long gone, rotted and razed, and the house was vacant up front. Nevertheless, my wife remembered the original, and I had made a promise.

Not long after moving in and starting work on the house, the lady next door came over to welcome us to the neighborhood. She had lived in our house as a child – she was nearing 100 years old by then - and remembered that porch, too. It must have been an extraordinary structure to still be etched into the minds of both her and my wife, I thought. If only I could picture it, too – I was the one who had to rebuild it, after all. Thankfully, in addition to greetings, our new neighbor came with so much more, what I needed all along: photos and drawings of our house, her childhood home, with that grand old porch sketched by an artist on paper for me to finally see. It was now real, an actual entity providing shelter and solace for multiple generations. If any were to be built, we all agreed then and there that it should match this one, the original porch, precisely.

Needless to say, I could not use the excuse that I did not know what the porch looked like, suddenly armed with black and white pictures and that artist's rendering in ink. In addition to their memories, I now had references; my promise took new priority. So I set about planning, measuring, sawing, building. Slowly, it took form.

The porch long lost on 53 Erie Street in Lancaster, New York has been reincarnated. Thanks to the memories of two women, total strangers now approach our home, ascend our stairs onto our front porch, and ring the bell. I will always let them take pictures and measurements; I dare not turn them away, nor withhold design ideas or suppliers. I may have built this porch, but it was always here, patiently awaiting rebirth.

* * *

"I can't take it no more, these mosquitoes are eating me alive!"

As much as I love being out here enjoying the nice air, talking and listening, silent sounds surrounding us, I'm once again overcome by these pesky little bloodsuckers. I even put the citronella candle directly underneath my porch rocker and they still eat me!

They don't seem to bother Pam, though. She just laughs at my whines, and when I ask her why they seem to prefer me, she says, *"Your blood is sweet."*

Intrigued, I ask, *"How does one get sweet blood?"* Then swat at another.

"You're Italian, Ange... Everyone loves Italian food..."

* * *

One of the drawbacks to having a nice old-fashioned porch, restored to the standards of the "good old days," is that if it is to be done correctly, it is to be made out of wood. Vinyl railings, spindles and posts need not apply! They were not yet invented in the good old days.

About every three years, our railings, spindles and posts need some TLC. They need to be scraped of any loose paint, sanded if need be, then primed and repainted. This is a job that is usually performed by Pam. She once said that, *"I was the one who wanted the porch like this so I'll paint it."* I never dissuade her.

The summer of 2004 has been terrible weather-wise. The National Weather Bureau said that this is the most gray and overcast July on record. Too much rain and humidity for priming and painting, so our porch maintenance had to be pushed back until the early part of August. As a result, Pam and I worked together this time, this year, priming the railings and spindles. We were already weeks late. So Pam turned on the television and tuned the satellite dish until finding one of the music stations: Classic Motown. Sweet soul music filled our ears and I went into the house, flipped-on the home theatre sound system, moved the speakers closer to the door, and cranked it up.

There was Sam and Dave, Aretha Franklin, Tower of Power, Otis Redding, Parliament, Sly and the Family Stone, even Michael Jackson, long before he was the King of Pop and living in Neverland. Inspired, our brushes dancing to the music, we almost didn't want the work to end, more railings and spindles, please, another song's about to start!

Like this old porch, classic music soothes the soul. Though this porch was Pam's idea, and the priming and painting her job, working together like this was a harmonious treat.

Too sweet not to share.

* * *

Pam and I were sitting on the porch on one of those summer nights when it is hot and sticky and nothing is moving. You couldn't buy a breeze tonight. It even seemed like the cars that passed by our house were going slower than normal. We were talking quietly, almost in whispers, sipping our beers.

It was so quiet that you could hear the ice cubes of a drink moving around, as that drink was sipped across the street.

Author's current home at 53 Erie Street prior to remodeling and "reincarnating" the former porch.

As I walk up the two steps to my porch, I look up at the dimmed-but-still-shiny brass numbers nailed symmetrically to the beam overhead. *5* and *3*: the numbers that represent our address. They are not just the numbers of our house, though, they were also the ages of our daughters when we moved in and made this our home.

My wife and daughters rewarded me with those numbers as a Father's Day gift that first year. The rehabbing was finally complete. I had put five months of massive work into this pre-Civil War house – the porch being only a minor task in comparison – and could have never done it without the help of family and friends, Labatts beer and sub sandwiches; the latter two perfect for bribing the former two. I believe it is a very nice home, much more than just a house.

There are many times that I look at the *5* and *3* and think back to what this place looked like without the front porch, like when we bought it at auction. And, as I look at those numbers, something else strikes me. I wish that I could turn back the clock to when Danie and Miko were still 5 and 3 years old. Their lives were overflowing with wonder and excitement.

This home was the first where they had bedrooms to call their own. It was a time when it was still okay for me to pick them up, hug them, hold them and kiss them on the head and *"smell their brains."* Squeezing me until my tongue stuck out and I started to choke, playing, faking, none of us wanted those hugs to end.

They are magical numbers: *5* and *3*, brass and human.

* * *

Becoming the Owner

In my lifetime of living out from under the roof of my parents, I have owned a condominium apartment, the house at 38 Brandel Avenue, and my current residence, 53 Erie Street. The condo needed practically no work prior to moving in. The house we lived in on Brandel Avenue required extensive rehabbing and renovation work, interior and exterior. The house at 53 Erie Street could be a book unto itself – and now literally is... Not only did it need a completely reconstructed porch, but just about everything else you could imagine to make it livable, comfortable.

The previous owners of 53 Erie Street had stopped making the mortgage payments for some time so the bank foreclosed on the property. Since the mortgage was federally backed, the house and lot became the property of the federal government. Payments unmade and taxes mounting, the bank decided to stop the bleeding on behalf of the government: Evicting the owners and their possessions, boarding up the house and putting a sign on the front warning anyone considering trespassing or tampering would have to answer to the FBI.

Working as the building inspector for the Village of Lancaster at that time, I was informed of the proceedings and witnessed the boarding-up of the house. When I contacted the Veterans Administration as to what was to become of it, they stated that in about six months the house and lot would be auctioned off in a sealed bid process. I was already accustomed to passing by this particular address – 53 Erie Street - many times a day and, over the next few months, grew fond of it for some reason. In hindsight, I wonder if maybe I wasn't looking for more abuse. Having recently finished an extensive rehab at 38 Brandel Avenue that would make even Bob Vila proud, but coming to realize that my growing family would soon outgrow our home, I was already antsy to tackle another.

I talked to Pam about asking a realtor to let us in to have a look. Understandably, she thought I was out of my mind. She too wondered why I wanted to put myself through that ordeal once again – more planning, gutting, sawing, pounding and finishing – but on a much grander scale this time. Even still, she did agree to a tour, and afterward to put in a bid; just as long as I rebuilt that porch *"the way it used to be."* Our bid was adequate, and we were suddenly the owners of a house with, as I would always say, potential.

The Preliminaries

Given Pam's initial reluctance on buying this house, then insistence on rebuilding that porch - and my subsequent promise - one of the first things I did was inspect the foundation along the front and side of 53 Erie Street; our new home. It was sorely lacking, cracking and missing basic supports for any porch, never mind the original. I quickly realized my task was going to be enormous. None of what existed could remain; in order to reconstruct the porch that Pam and our neighbor remembered, I would have to start fresh: a complete rebuild to present-day code and zoning laws. Being the building inspector, I knew the many daunting restrictions chapter and verse, but now I was also a contractor and carpenter. Needless to say, I was fully cognizant that all I did from hereon would come under great scrutiny. From the very start, with Pam's memories and my politically appointed position, I had far too many supervisors.

The first impediment was the front-yard setback requirement of twenty-five feet. On my street, the village actually owns a "right of way" of thirty feet in each direction from the center of the road. Other than sidewalks and grass, nothing can be built in this area. Given the dimensions of 53 Erie Street and my designs, there could be no porch whatsoever – The village's laws were explicit, and I was employed to uphold them. The fact that there once was a porch didn't help either; if a structure does not exist for over one year, it could not be rebuilt under a grandfather clause. I could always apply for a variance, but as the building inspector, that would be highly suspect if the village zoning board of appeals ruled in my favor.

Deterred yet undaunted, I continued to look for any loophole, but also prepared to break the news to Pam. Sorry, there can be no porch; our reason for bidding on this home was moot.

Then, just in the nick of time, I found one regulation - seldom used but still law - permitting an addition to the front of a house as long as it protrudes into the right of way and extends no further than any existing houses in the area. Here, among assorted arcane ordinances, I had found my salvation.

Pam's porch could be built!

From the Ground Up

Like a house, a porch needs to have the proper foundation. Being in the Buffalo area, as infamous for blizzards and long thaws as anywhere in America, the soil will freeze in most winters to a depth of three feet. Therefore, the foundation needs to be at or close to that depth: a measurement known as the *"frost line."* Being below the frost line will prevent a structure from heaving up as the ground freezes and expands. Stable, a porch must be as solid as the house it is attached to, and the depth of its foundation is critical, here and most other places.

Seven holes were dug down to forty-two inches – three feet plus six inches for good measure - each hole being eight inches in diameter. Pouring a few shovels of concrete into the holes, five foot long, four by four-inch square pressure-treated (water-resistant) posts were then pounded downward. These wooden framing members now standing vertical, the hole was then filled with more concrete, to just below ground level. This left about two feet of post protruding from the ground, later to be cut to the necessary height, and all of them were checked for "plumb" or absolute vertical with a level, then braced until the concrete set-up.

The Floor System

Most people call the portion of the porch that they stand on *"the floor"* or *"deck."* Many mistakenly think that this is the most important part of a porch; it is the most apparent, but hardly as critical as the underlying system. Floorboards are easily pulled-up and replaced, but what holds them in place is essential. The structure just beneath the floor or deck, to which the boards are nailed or screwed to, is known as *"the floor joist system,"* while the outer frame of the floor joist system is called *"the band joist frame."* This frame rested upon or was directly attached to our new posts in the concrete and ground. Since it is a complete frame, a portion of it – known as *"the ledger board"* – was actually attached to the house.

On my porch, the floor joist system is constructed of two-inch by eight-inch pressure-treated lumber attached to the ledger board and the outside frame, making up *"the floor joist."* Each was nailed in place, parallel to each other, sixteen inches apart. Inside a house, the floor system is constructed to be "level" or at absolute horizontal, but on a porch a little bit of an angle is built in, to help water run-off away the house, toward the front and sides of the porch.

The Floor

Most porch floors in northeastern America are constructed of pinewood boards measuring two and one-quarter inches wide and one and one-eighth inch thick. The boards have a tongue running along one edge and a groove along the other, allowing the groove of one board to inter-lock with the tongue of the board adjacent to it. The boards are nailed to the floor joist through the tongue, and when another board is placed against it, the procedure is repeated. This means a tight and secure floor with no nails showing.

However, when I was pricing out the materials for my porch floor, a friend of mine who owned a small lumber company recommended Philippine Mahogany. I questioned his sanity, but humored him anyway and asked for price. He did – and to my amazement – using mahogany for the entire floor was only seventeen dollars more! Even still, mahogany? I was building a porch, not antique furniture... *"Ange, they build boats out of mahogany."* my friend said, and I was sold.

I then visited some homeowners who already had mahogany floors, questioned them about it and came away quite surprised at the durability of the wood. I was told that I'd have to refinish it every two years with an oil-based finish, which withstands all the sun and snow that a Western New York summer and winter can heap upon it. This was a small trade-off for a floor with a golden brown-orange tone versus the alternative: plastered with stain or paint.

Mahogany it was.

The Structure Overhead

My porch is an "L" configuration, measuring seven feet by twenty-two feet in each direction. Because of this design, a *"hip roof"* system was to be utilized. In order to construct a roof system, a frame similar to the band joist frame of the floor is used.

Just as with the floor system, a series of *"ceiling joists"* performed much the same function as the floor joists.   The ceiling joists will hold the actual ceiling of the porch, just as the floor joists do the deck. Like their function, building the roof system is similar to the floor, and also has to be supported during construction. Since I did not yet have the posts that would support the roof system, a temporary system of supports was used to mimic the real posts. Regular spruce pine fir lumber was used in the fabrication, then removed and replaced by the real posts at the very end.

Inclined, the top of the porch roof has a series of *"rafters"* that are attached to the frame portion of the roofing system - again attached to the house ledger board like the floor joists. These rafters proceed in a downward slope until resting atop the roof system frame, sitting in a notch called a *"bird's mouth"* that is cut into each rafter to allow them to fit nicely upon the frame. As in almost all construction, the spacing of the rafters is sixteen inches apart.

The porch ceiling is made of one-quarter inch thick Luan Mahogany plywood sheets. Unlike the floor, though, the ceiling will be painted white. The porch roof is constructed of five-eighths-inch thick exterior grade plywood covered with felt paper then asphalt shingles.

All that is left to do is attach the trim boards and gutters and you have a porch roof.

Going Up and Across

Although I had promised Pam to restore the porch as it was when she was young, modern technology and materials actually afforded me to do it a bit better. It would never be exactly the same – What is? - But newer, maybe more reminiscent than any full replacement of the original. Still, I did remain faithful, and the porch was now ready for the real posts and complementary railing and spindle system. So I looked and looked for porch posts as close to those in our neighbor's pictures and Pam's mind. I wanted to honor my oath, but these posts and spindles – each elaborate yet essential for holding-up the roofing system - were quite expensive. Since I needed over one hundred spindles and six posts, I balked at the price time and again, but kept reminding myself of that promise to Pam.

My Uncle John used to own a grocery with my Dad and delivered groceries in the Blasdell area. This may seem totally unrelated, but my Uncle John was also a shrewd businessman. He's the one who found this little nondescript lumberyard on the outskirts of Buffalo and told me about their wide assortment. Still balking at the prices for spindles and posts, I picked the ones I wanted from a brochure then let Uncle John negotiate with the lumberyard. Repeatedly telling the proprietor *"To sharpen the pencil a bit more.*" Uncle John got me the best prices available. Whether groceries or spindles, few people ever walked away from a deal with Uncle John.

Spindles and posts purchased, our only other struggle was the railings. Unfortunately, any commercially available railings did not fit into the scheme of the porch design. So I made the top and bottom railings out of Douglas fir, two by four-inch lumber, and Pam helped run the electric router, giving the edges some detail, character. Once finished, each post was placed directly atop the mahogany floorboards, resting atop the band joist system atop the posts protruding from the concrete and ground, and all of it attached to both the roof and frame of the house. Before finally, officially, securing each post, they were checked for plumb, and all of the temporary posts removed. Our porch was taking form, now standing on its own, and the railings and spindles were cut to size and attached between each post.

Dressing It All Off

Just as a prim and proper lady might wear a skirt or an apron, a porch should be adorned with the same. Keeping to the theme of the original porch, pressure treated *"lattice panels"* were used to cover the nether regions, from the floorboards to the ground. The lattice was attached to the posts and the band joist system, so as to seem to float just above the earth. The panels were then trimmed-out with pressure-treated lumber and a small trim was added to complete the scheme. All our porch lacked was paint.

Hats Off to Wayne and Dad

Obviously, the construction of this porch could not have been a success without the help of others. In addition to Pam, our neighbor and Uncle John, it might not have been even possible if not for the efforts and fine craftsmanship of my good buddy Wayne Shafer. He is a carpenter without peer, and executed all of my design ideas to perfection. When I offered him a drawing or sketch, he would either tell me to *"Shove the drawings where the moon don't shine."* or that *"I don't need no stinkin' plans!"* Or, more often, Wayne would simply say, *"Just tell me what you want and stay the Hell out of the way..."* He is a dear friend and character larger than life. His toil has been repaid over the years, as we have sat on this porch sipping a few fine Labatts beverages, sharing stories: our ritual and privilege.

My Dad was with Wayne every step of the construction, replacing me entirely when I was at work. If you were to ask Dad what he did, he'd go on forever telling you how he did this and that. You'd think he built the whole porch himself!

But if you were to ask Wayne to sum-up Dad's role, his response is more diplomatic: *"I couldn't have done it without Tony."*

* * *

Pam told me that I have no taste. Specifically, she said that I had no sense of what porch hand railings should look like. The wrought-iron railings on the steps that I was prepping to paint looked like "Bobbie-pins" to her, and I argued back that they fit the house perfectly.

"The only thing perfect about them is that they are perfectly ugly."

Well, I won this one by telling her that I would not replace them with what she wanted, because these wrought-iron railings were here when we bought the house. So I continued with the prepping and priming, then painted them black to contrast with the two blues and russet colors of the house.

I may have a change of heart someday, but today, they do not look like Bobbie-pins. They look like they belong. Someday, maybe, I will drive by this house and see whether or not the next owners agree.

If these wrought-iron railings are gone, then as Pam said, I have no taste.

* * *

I am a teacher.

Actually, I have been for most of my working life: Teaching in Hawaii for years, then moving back to Western New York and having to find another job until a position opened up at one of the local schools. After serving as the building inspector for the village, and having my fill of positions picked by politicians, I became a remodeling contractor, and also worked as a cabinetmaker, commercial millwork project manager, as well as a middle school teacher. I am now a Technology Education Teacher at Orchard Park High School and have held this post for over five years. Whether instructing students how to master assorted wood and construction technologies, home maintenance and repair, or segues into graphic arts and digital photography, I love my job, and I'll tell you why.

I have no job, no cause to labor, between the end of June and early September. I still get up early, joining my neighbors every morning, sending them off to their jobs. From my porch, sitting back in my chair, I hoist my coffee cup high in salute. And they all wave back, signaling to one another to have a good day. To only myself, though, I am acknowledging that this is my reward for spending many long days, nights, and weekends in the classroom, or working in my den, making lesson plans and grading papers. For these three months I am free, a professional porch sitter, but for the other nine, I am in the classroom, preparing, teaching and tutoring.

My classroom is somewhat different than most because mine is a lab full of machines that require time-consuming repairs and set-up for the next day's lessons and demonstrations. So, while I am in school on Saturdays, my neighbors are at home. And while I am grading papers at night, my neighbors are at leisure. It is a trade-off, we all exchange our time and energy for different reasons, but, sitting here on my porch thinking about it, I bet that my neighbors and I actually spend the same amount of time at work each year. The sole difference being that my break is more compacted, covering the summer, and certainly more noticeable, with me perpetually on my porch, hoisting my coffee cup high.

I can understand why people would get jealous, almost angry, seeing me sitting, spending many a summer morning on my porch. And, whenever someone says something snide like *"There's my tax dollars at work..."* I can only laugh.

For nine months each year, teachers as a whole spend more time with children than their parents do. And, if they were to try it, they would need several months of porch therapy, too.

* * *

Today is a gorgeous July afternoon. I just finished cutting the grass and trimming the lawn along the edge of the sidewalk. These are two things that Pam says I am anal about.

Sitting here, resting, just watching the traffic going by, this is the prime time to jot down some more memories. So I went into the house and got my laptop computer and brought it outside. Opening the case, I looked at the computer, then mused at how amazing, empowering, technology is. Just a handful of years ago, this would not have been possible. I'd be in the house at the desktop computer doing this. Now I can just sit here in the warmth of the summer breeze, immersed in the great outdoors. All I need is a spot to put the laptop.

Ironically, laps aren't the best places for laptops: they are cumbersome, as unpredictable as the people they are attached to. I gave some thought to dragging the coffee table from the living room out onto the porch, but that would almost be like I was still inside the house. So I looked around and decided that I would put the laptop on the seat of the porch swing. Dragging a chair up to the swing, I was ready to go. Did the inventors of laptop technology ever envision this? A person perched on a porch being productive...

* * *

Our neighbor, located diagonally across the street from us, is sitting on her porch with her daughter and her dog. She occasionally brings the dog outside and ties its leash to one of the porch step handrails. When the dog is inside the house, you can see it poking its head through the curtains of the front windows to see outside.

From where I sit on my porch I can see two familiar joggers exercising their dog. As is the law in Lancaster, dogs must be restrained by leash when they are not fenced-in. Their dog is on a leash. The neighbor's dog, also leashed to the handrails, has not seen the other dog approaching. It will very shortly, and the melee will begin again.

I have seen and heard it countless times from my porch. The barking and yelping of the neighbor's dog when another dog passes in front of its house, not making any difference whether or not the other dog is on this or that side of the street. The dog pays little if any attention to squirrels or cats when they make an appearance, only other dogs. I wonder why that is?

If a dog has never seen itself in a mirror, how does it know what it looks like? How does it know what species or breed it is, how large or small? That might explain why a little dog does not fear or back down from a bigger dog in a confrontation. If a dog doesn't know what it looks like, then how does it know to bark at other dogs?

* * *

I've been trying to watch what I eat this summer because of high cholesterol and triglyceride numbers. Oftentimes I find myself with fruit smoothies to drink and raisins, grapes and walnuts to snack on. Being in the mood for a late morning snack, I filled the bowl with munchies and opted for watching the impending rain-showers from the porch.

I looked at the walnuts individually before popping them into my mouth, noting whether or not they were whole or in pieces. I can't help but notice the aroma of each nut. The smell sends my thoughts back to the Christmas holidays when I was growing up, working at Uncle

John's and Dad's Italian grocery store, Swan Importing. Behind the counter, where the people waited while their groceries were tallied up, there were always open boxes of mixed nuts: walnuts, filberts, almonds, and brazil nuts available for sale by the pound.

I can still see in my mind's eye the nutcracker hanging from a nail under the counter. I would grab a nut now and then, crack it open and pop it into my mouth. The walnut was the most challenging of the lot because I would invariably break the nut inside into little pieces while cracking the shell. I'd then have to use the little shiny steel nut pick to get the pieces out. The pick was stored under the counter in a cigar box, along with the screwdrivers, pliers, and a bottle opener.

Uncle Joey, my Mom's and Uncle John's younger brother, occasionally worked at the grocery store on his days off. His regular job was at the beef house, where he would carry quarter- or half-sides of cows from the butcher room to the refrigerated trucks. There he would impale them on big stainless steel hooks that hung from the roofs of the trucks. The beef was then delivered to small butcher shops that catered to the public.

Uncle Joey stood about five-foot-five and weighed well over two hundred pounds. He could have doubled for Don Corleone, the character that Marlon Brando played in the *"Godfather"* movies. He was small by most beef handler standards, but all muscle, except for his belly that hung out just a bit. The most memorable part of Uncle Joey's physical appearance was his hands. When I was small they seemed to be the size of basketballs. The thumbs were so short that they seemed to be just an outcropping of the palm. His fingers were also short, but incredibly thick, like individual bananas.

I remember Uncle Joey snatching the nutcracker out of my hand and hanging it back up on the nail. He smiled and said, *"Watch me, I'm going to show you how to open walnuts like a man."* Putting one walnut in the palm of his right hand along his lifeline, he then put another walnut on top of it, perpendicular, ninety-degrees to his lifeline and the walnut below. Walnuts in place, he made a fist, then punched it into his left hand, just once, two fists colliding. Opening his palm, he revealed the walnuts: one was split in half, opened wide, the nuts inside perfectly intact. I asked him to show me again and he did, with the same result.

I tried innumerable times but my little hand couldn't close around the two walnuts; I couldn't fashion the necessary fist to punch my other. As I grew older, taller, stronger, I was able to break walnuts in this way, but I never managed to keep the nuts inside from breaking into little pieces. As my girls were growing up, I used to impress them with this little trick around the Christmas holidays. They never minded that the actual nuts inside were broken; only I knew of Uncle Joey's precision.

Even though he worked in the beef processing plant, with the proper training, Uncle Joey could have been a boxer. It is alleged that, in his younger days, he beat up a kid in a street fight who went on to earn some prominence in the lower weight divisions as a professional boxer. When you were around Uncle Joey, you had the feeling that no harm could ever come to you. I don't think he feared any man. I often wondered what he would have done to any robber who dared come into the grocery store, even if they had a gun.

Uncle Joey once instructed me on how to conduct myself if I was ever in a fight with a stranger, as well as what to do if I ever got into a fight with someone that I knew and might see again. He said the former was like fighting for your life and the latter was fighting to preserve your honor. The major difference between the two was how the first fifteen seconds of either fight plays out. A cruel and painful difference... Unlike Uncle Joey's early days of street fighting on the East Side of Buffalo, my life in South Buffalo was more placid. I had a fight now and then, but they all seemed to be with or against friends so I never needed to use one of the tactics he taught me for strangers. I won't share it here, either, for fear of giving anyone advice that might be used in the wrong way, under all the wrong circumstances.

It is amazing though, how breaking, smelling, looking at, then eating a nut about one inch in length while sitting on my porch during a rainstorm, can cause me to remember that strong little man with massive hands. He showed and taught me more than a few things in and about life, and cracking walnuts by-hand is just one that I still have not mastered to this day.

* * *

It's about 5:45 a.m. and, other than a few passing cars carrying people on their way to work, it seems like the world belongs to me. I'm sitting here on the porch wearing shorts and a t-shirt, sipping from a cup of coffee that seems to taste and smell better than usual. The sun hasn't decided whether or not it is going to come up or just hide behind the overcast clouds to start the day. It's already hot and muggy and it seems like nothing is moving. It's not the best way to begin the day weather-wise but the perfect way for me.

Being awake and outdoors hours before any of my neighbors makes me feel like I own the morning and have a jump on the day. I take in the songs of the early birds, especially the cardinals, who have beautiful lullabies. I watch the baby squirrels chase each other around the tree, screeching and clawing up the bark, stopping occasionally in dead stillness, then continuing their game of chase.

I can feel this way because I have no place to be. No need to drive a car anywhere. All I have to do is sip this cup of coffee. And then I hear something, a rather troubling sound for so early in the morning. It's the sound of a bass system, coming from an imported car passing by. *"Bump-Da-Bump!"* shattering the splendid silence.

Though the car isn't near, I give the driver a disgusted look anyway, and ask, *"How can anyone stand music that loud?"* It doesn't even seem like actual music, just blaring, disturbing noise. After the car passes I can still hear and feel the percussion as it goes up the street.

For a short time, I felt that the morning belonged only to me, with its sounds of birds and squirrels and tires on pavement. Now the stillness has been broken by noise coming from an expensive audio system that's probably worth more than the car itself.

I'm sure the squirrels heard that noise coming from that car, too.

When's the last time that driver heard squirrels?

* * *

Pam and I were sitting on the porch and all of a sudden we heard a thump, thump... We looked toward the noise and saw that one of our neighbor's cats had been run over by a car. The car didn't bother to stop. Not the screech of brakes or honk of a horn, only that sickening thump, thump...

We looked at each other. *"Did you see that?"* we seemed to be saying without speaking.

Beyond that cat lying lifeless in the middle of the road, the saddest thing about it is that I felt no pity or remorse. I'm sure this sounds cold, but the people who own those cats aren't good neighbors. They have never controlled their cats: allowing them to wander the neighborhood and use other peoples' properties as their litter boxes. They kill our shrubs, urinate on our house siding and car tires, get into the garbage and leave their crap all over our lawns and gardens. Not just ours' but any adjacent neighbors', too. We have spoken to them about their cats multiple times, but their reply is always the same. *"Well, what can we do? They sometimes get out of our yard!"*

We had a cat for fourteen years and never had these problems. It was always inside, only rarely escaped, and never tormented or marred our neighbors. I guess that's my justification for not feeling sorry for this cat, this time.

Pam is more humanitarian, and went across the street to tell the neighbors that their cat had been run over by a car. Sad to admit, but if I were alone tonight, sitting on the porch and hearing that thump thump... I wouldn't have bothered.

* * *

This is my last day of summer, sitting on the porch, drinking coffee and reading the newspaper. School starts tomorrow. I'm always ready to go back, but this year I'm just a little bit apprehensive. I spent a lot of time this summer working on material for a new course I'll be teaching. I keep wondering if I did a good enough job of preparing for it, knowing that I'll be taking it public in a few days.

I'm also mindful of the fact that this might be the last day of summer for many of the seniors that graduated in June from the high school. Tomorrow will be their first taste of "reality education" - where no one holds your hand and gives you extra chances to turn in work that is late. It will be the first time they won't need a note from their parents if they don't go to class; for most of them, their time management skills are going to be put to the test. There will be no reports every five weeks to keep their parents informed of their progress or lack thereof. In fact, if they are no longer considered a minor, their parents can't even get information from the college or university they might be attending. For too many, there will just be the hard, cold reality of instant failure.

With all of this in mind, I assure myself that I tried my best to inform them about the "real world" that awaits them the day after they take off their graduation cap and gown. It all begins, and ends, tomorrow.

* * *

Today was a gorgeous autumn day. I came home from school, cut the grass and rewarded myself with a nice cold LaBatts Blue. Just before sitting down and taking my first sip, I unfurled the flag that we have always flown from our porch. It was twisted around the pole because of the high winds and I helped it hang with honor once more, gently flapping in the breeze.

For some reason, I then looked up and down the street and noticed that there were more flags flying from porch posts than I can ever recall seeing. 9-11. A few weeks ago, our lives were changed forever. All of a sudden there was a tremendous run on flags at all of the stores. Everybody wanted to display his or her patriotism. We have always had a flag, I guess as a carryover from my in-laws; it's just something that we have always done. Today, though, it's simply awe inspiring to see so many flags flapping from front porches.

It is a little sad, too. To think that it took an act of terrorism to cause this outpouring of national pride. The sale and display of so many American flags, here and all across the country, seems to be the rage now that we've been reminded what we have, and could lose so quickly. America is still the best deal going when it comes to almost everything, but I don't think everyone knows or truly appreciates that.

Standing there, looking down a street lined with red, white and blue, I flashed back to the morning that I yelled at my homeroom class in school when they were talking during the Pledge of Allegiance. I told them that a lot of people gave their lives so they could be here, doing what they were doing, so shut-up and show some respect! It's the same as now.

I wonder how many of these flags will be standing in the months and years to come? Mine has always been here, anyone who has passed by my house, any house I have owned, can attest to that. But, will some of these flags become dirty or tattered, desecrated by neglect, twisted around their poles and ignored? Will their owners know to take them down? Will they then be replaced by another, newer, American flag?

How long will this outpouring of patriotism last? I really wonder...

* * *

We had some really nice weather, considering it's December and Buffalo. I retrieved all of the Christmas decorations from the garage and put them on the front porch, where they will spend the next three to four weeks, weather and spirit permitting. I was never one to get carried away with the whole decorating scene during the holidays, but feel that a house with a porch as nice as ours should at least have a splash of color.

I don't ever remember my parents' house being decorated. My father is somewhat a Scrooge. *"I don't want nothing from no one and I'm not buying anything for anyone..."* was his favorite seasons greeting. He has said that from when I was a little kid until today. His other quote, which he used on my mother a lot, was, *"Anna, you're going to get the same thing you got last year, only in a bigger box."*

I never wanted to be like my father around the holidays. I wanted to provide my daughters a little bit of Xmas color and cheer and have been putting up a few things on the porch ever since they were old enough to remember.

A few of our neighbors go all out with grand displays. I use the simple approach of two internally illuminated candles and a stand-up Santa set aglow. So they don't blow over from the winds and weather, I tie the candles to two of the porch posts with kite twine. The Santa stands on his own well enough but occasionally falls over because of the winds, his barrel-belly rolling around on the porch floor until the bulb inside breaks and he goes dark. I touch it all off with large and small red ribbons tied to all of the posts. The lights and ribbons are simple but create a very cheery entrance to the front door. It's enchanting for me to drive down the street, pause to look at our porch, then pull into our driveway at the end of the day.

Taking the decorations down at the end of the holidays is always depressing for me. It's the same feeling I get when we bring the porch furniture into the basement for the winter.

Author's childhood home at 193 Sheffield Avenue.

We got yelled at, big time! My brother Tony and I, along with some of our friends, were sitting on the front porch shooting the bull. Our father came out from the back yard where he was doing some work on the car. He looked up to see who was on the porch with us and then he started to yell like a lunatic.

Dad was upset that we all had our feet up on the front railing. He accused us of not caring about how hard he worked to make the rails look that nice. Enraged, he wasn't really yelling at any of us in particular, *"That's what's wrong with you kids today! You don't give a damn about anything anybody does or how hard anybody works to make things nice... Now get your damned feet off of the railing or go home!"*

Boldly, I barked back, *"I'll bet that in twenty or thirty years when me and Tony and our friends are no longer around, you'll give anything to have us all back here on the porch, putting our feet up on your railing..."*

* * *

My brother and I ate supper really fast, knowing that it was going to be our regular Saturday night routine. Almost every summer Saturday night, we went to the stock car races at Civic Stadium. We ate too fast, though, and had to wait and waste some time before our father told us to get ready to leave. Then he asked if we wanted to take a friend along this week.

I went to our friend Chet's house and sat outside on the porch while he ran inside to plead with his mother to let him go. After lots of yelling, he came out on the porch, sat down and cursed his mother for saying no. I told him that we would try again some other Saturday night. Sitting there with him, waiting for Dad to call me home, I thought about how lucky we were to have a father that took us to the races. Me and Dad and Tony and sometimes Uncle Frank would all go. We would park at Aunt Nicky's house only a few blocks from Civic Stadium then walk from there. As we approach-ed the stadium I could smell the burning rubber and gas fumes; I could hear the tires squealing as the cars sped around the turns; the loud roar of the motors that sounded like they would explode at any moment.

We walked through the entrance tunnel and fol-lowed Dad to his favorite seat, which was actually a wooden bleacher. Spreading out the old green-pea-colored Army blanket, we took our seats and watched the cars run warm-up laps then return to the pits. After a while, the cars at last started to roll out for their heats. Dad would look at the pit tunnel and count off the cars in pairs of two. *"Holy Christ! There's eighteen cars in this heat!"*

Dad then asked us what number car we picked and we told one another, watching them roll past, gaining speed. Rounding the track, taking a few pace laps, we could feel the breeze stir up, exhaust fumes filling the air, engulfing us.

"Ladies and gentlemen, here they come down the backstretch..." The announcer would shout over the PA system, *"They're wheel to wheel, fender to fender, hub to hub and... They're off!"*

After the race started we couldn't hear a word he said, drown-out by the roaring engines. This night was as exciting as any, but with one major exception. We saw a racecar driver die in front of our eyes.

His car spun out and hit the wall sideways. He tried to get out of the car - it was in a spot where other cars could slam into it - and he crawled out of the passenger-side window, struggling to climb up the concrete wall to safety. Before he could get to the top of the wall, his disabled car was hit by another car and he was crushed.

The stadium went silent.

The announcer was saying things, anything, trying to take everyone's minds off what we had all just witnessed.

"Is he dead Dad?" we asked a thousand times, *"Dad, is he dead?"*

Dad never answered.

We would go to the stock car races plenty more times after that night. But it would never be the same.

* * *

Dad told Tony and me that we had to go with him to visit Grandma and Grandpa Daluisio today. We always hated visiting them because it was so boring. They were nice grandparents but there was nothing to do at their house.

They lived on Bailey Avenue: a main street in Buffalo that was very busy and noisy with traffic, day and night. Their yard was tiny and there wasn't room enough to do much at all. They had grumpy neighbors on one side and a used car lot on the other. In the winter we just stayed in the house and watched TV with Grandpa. His favorite television show was the Red Skeleton Hour. He used to laugh so hard that he would literally cry. In the summer we would throw a tennis ball around in their postage stamp of a yard, ever careful to not throw too hard and lose our only ball to those angry neighbors or among all those used cars.

Most of the time, though, we would just sit on their tiny, elevated, concrete porch and watch the traffic go by.

Their porch had wrought iron railings with three and sometimes four metal chairs on it. Directly across Bailey Avenue was a business called Buffalo Sectional Homes; for years while sitting on that porch in the summertime, I would watch and wait for a home to emerge from the giant overhead doors along the front of that red brick building. I never saw even one. I did see many big boxes wrapped in white paper on the back of flatbed trucks, but no houses ever came out. Heck, I never even saw a single garage or shed come out of that building!

After a few years of watching and waiting, I figured that the business was a front for something illegal. The Mafia has always been active in Buffalo, and I imagined all the shady deals going down just over Bailey. I never wanted to ask my father about it because I didn't want him to think I was dumb, that I couldn't figure things out on my own. So, one day, I got brave and told my father that I was going to go across the street to take a look for myself. The garage doors were open and I crept close, then saw it all.

Inside, I saw houses and garages being built in small sections. The sections were wrapped in white paper, then put onto flatbed trucks. They actually were building houses and garages in pieces in there, then taking them away on a truck for assembly elsewhere. Buffalo Sectional

Homes, it all made sense... *What a great idea*, I thought to myself. And then I thought, yes indeed, I am dumb. Not dumb because I couldn't figure it out, but because I feared asking my father what the workers did in the building across the street from Grandma and Grandpa.

Many years later, taking Danie somewhere, I had occasion to drive up Bailey Avenue past Grandma and Grandpa's former home. Their house had burned down, so I pointed to where it used to stand and said to my daughter that this is where my Grandma and Grandpa used to live. In the same breath, I then pointed to that red brick building and said that they used to build pieces of houses inside of there and drive them out on trucks. Buffalo Sectional Homes is no longer in business, but Danie took her thumb out of her mouth, leaned forward in her car seat, and looked at me. Puzzled, staring out the window at that red brick building, she said amazed, *"No way, Papa..."*

* * *

Twenty-one years ago Dad asked me to send my friend, who was a carpet installer, over to his house on Sheffield Avenue. The purpose was to give my father an estimate on putting "astroturf" carpeting on his porch floor.

Hearing this, I yelled, *"Why would anyone in their right mind put plastic, grass-like carpet on their porch?"*

"It'll look nice and I won't have to paint it anymore" he replied. Incensed, I told him that, if God meant for porch floors to have grass on them, he would have made grass grow on horizontal wooden surfaces instead of out of the soil. In response, he quipped, *"Someday you'll know what it's like to have to paint a porch floor every couple of years."*

Dad was never afraid to spend his money on the best. His theory was to "go first class" and buy something of good quality and not to have to worry about replacing it anytime soon. So, in his fine "first class" fashion, he bought the best astroturf available back then, paying as much for it as some of the best carpeting you could for the inside of your house.

Twenty-one years later, as I sit here today on his porch, then lay flat on my back, head resting on the soft floor, I run my hands, palm side down, over the astroturf. It feels as good today as it did when it was installed way back then.

Sitting nearby in his chair, Dad must have been reading my mind, because he leaned over and looked me square in the eyes, smiling that *"I told you so..."* smile.

"*You thought I was crazy didn't you?*" He asked, rhetorically of course, adding, "*But I was right, wasn't I?*"

Laying there, enjoying Dad's astroturf porch, I smiled back at him, then admitted, disgusted, "*Yea Dad, I believed you were crazy... But I now know you're right.*"

Sometimes it pays to "go first class."

Pam's childhood home, 37 Erie Street.

It's about midnight right now and July 5th. It is the hottest day of the summer so far. The weathermen say it could be a record year for heat.

Pam and I were married today. We are at my new wife's parents' house – I have in-laws now. The reception is over but we decided to hang around their house instead of rushing off on a honeymoon. We will leave for Hawaii in two days to start our new life together. Hawaii is where I work, teaching high school. I guess you might say that Hawaii - our destination and Pam's new home - will be a honeymoon unto itself; a permanent one at that.

Pam is in the house talking to her family and I am on the porch. I am lying on my back on the wide rail looking up at the sky, just thinking. Reflecting on the wedding and reception and how much fun we had. Pam in her hot pants and Afro wig, me in my smiley face tie and bell-bottoms. Music from the musical *"Hair"* and vows written personally by us were all parts of this day, our day, as were our great friends.

Our wedding was strange by most peoples' standards but, by ours', it was ideal. Everyone had a blast. The musicians were a black band. Just the thought of African-Americans at an Italian wedding had my Grandma threatening to not come.

My cousin passed out from too much beer; my brother's godfather threw up and lost his false teeth in the dark behind the fire hall. Someone got a speeding ticket on the way to the reception... All in all, a great time was had by all.

My last thought of many tonight, while lying on the porch railing is this.... I wonder how many grooms spend their wedding night lying on their backs, on a wide porch railing looking up at the stars?

* * *

Pam's dad, I called him Pop, and Jack, his next door neighbor, invited me up on the porch to help them empty a few quart bottles of Simon Pure beer. It was a typical Western New York summer evening, hot and humid, but better than any Western New York winter.

Pop always called me Swinger. In fact, he called everyone Swinger. He would say, *"Swinger, will thee join us in partaking of the magic potion?"*

I never had to answer.

Pop drank his beer out of a small glass that jelly used to come in. Not a mason jar, no, something unique, like him. Pop referred to it as the professional drinker's glass, small and cute, and easily emptied with a few big swallows. And, after emptying another, he would set it down on the little round table and give a sigh of pleasure. Over time, my daughters would come to imitate him and give sighs of their own after they drank something good. Thanks to Pop, satisfied sighs have become a mainstay in our family.

After a few short moments, Pop looked at his empty jar and asked Jack if he drank the beer. As usual, Jack answered no – Jack doesn't drink alcohol, everyone knows that – but Pop continued to question him about the missing beer anyway. Jack always denied it, but Pop always grilled him. Finally, Pop refilled the jelly jar then tells Jack that he is watching him. Eyes focused until that jelly jar is raised, another heavy gulp, Pop then looks at me, no need for suspicion here; my beer's almost empty.

"Swinger, you keep an eye on Jack... I have my doubts about his integrity."

And that jelly jar is again emptied, a professional practicing his trade; satisfied sighs followed by snickers.

* * *

Today I sat on the swing and just swung back and forth, listening to the sound of the chain links hanging it from the ceiling rubbing against each other. Today is so much more than just another day of swinging on the porch, though. This time I'm holding my daughter Danie, just a baby, now almost 1½ years old.

I looked at her as she slept. Her little lips were puckered as if she was going to kiss someone. Because of the heat and humidity, little beads of sweat form on her forehead and around her little button nose. I'm glad she didn't get my Italian nose.

My life is so different because of this little person. I might someday drive by this house, many years from now, and look at it as the one that we used to live in. Not some other family's, ours'. This porch, this swing, anchored to ceiling, big nickel-plated hooks squeaking. I will always remember swinging my baby to sleep.

Author's, and his family's, first home
(and first fixer-upper) at 38 Brandel Avenue.
Picture taken prior to rehab.

I've been looking forward to this day for a long time. The weather has finally turned a bit warmer and most of the interior renovation and rehab work is complete, except for a few minor items. Since we first bought this house on Brandel Avenue, I've been planning on removing the wooden framed glass windows from the front porch. This style of porch, in this geographic area, is often referred to as a "sunroom" or "sun porch." Through this process of transformation, it will become an open-air porch, letting in the air, wind, sounds and scents of the neighborhood. I viewed what I was about to do as freeing the soul of the porch.

The previous owners were not very handy with power tools, so as a result, the entire house had fallen into disrepair. We pretty much gutted the entire first floor and, starting with basically just the outside shell, transformed the once boxy-looking interior into a bright, wide-open area. Gone were the floor-to-ceiling walls that divided the space into rooms. In their place now stood half walls, pass-thrus and boxed beams. The interior of the house has now taken on a modern, contemporary air, but the exterior still held fast to the farmhouse style.

As I began putting crowbar, wonderbar and hammer to good use on the wood frames of the sun porch, I tried hard not to break the glass that the frames enclosed. I did this in order to make the job of the garbage collectors a bit easier. It might also make the windows more attractive to garbage pickers and salvagers once they are placed out to the curb for collection.

As expected, not too long into the demolition work, a man came by in a car, got out and came up to the porch to ask if I was going to toss those windows? He said he had driven by the house many times and saw the lights on late at night and heard the buzzing of saws and banging of hammers. I admitted that I was the culprit. He then asked if I could save the porch windows for him for a few days, promising to return with a pickup truck to take them away? Could he give me a few dollars for my trouble? I told him that I didn't want any money for the windows but I was pleased to know that they would be put to good use.

Later on, I had all of the windows removed from the north side of the porch when one of the neighbors from across the street came over. He introduced himself as Art and welcomed us to the neighborhood. He commented on all of the work that he had seen completed since we bought the house, but wondered why I would want to remove the glass, as he felt that, *"The windows give the porch of sense of homey-ness."*

Even though this was the first time we had officially met and conversed, the first time I had actually seen Art was back in May. When we were moving into this house. He was one of several of our yet-to-be-met neighbors, among the many who came out to watch the spectacle that I created when I tore the top off of our U-Haul van.

In my defense, I was used to driving a MGB convertible while renting that van to move all of our worldly possessions into our new house. MGB's are small and agile, and I had never been concerned about any type of overhead clearance. Therein was the potential for disaster.

As I approached the house, I was slowing down in order to park along the curb to pick up a few things. Not realizing it, the top corner of the van behind the passenger seat was headed for the low-hanging tree limb. With dead accuracy and precision, the corner of the van caught the tree limb and, the next thing I knew, the truck came to a crashing stop. My face slammed into the steering wheel and my right cheek swelled rapidly.

Gary, who was sitting in the passenger seat, jumped out to survey the damage. He looked above where he sat and said, *"I think you hit a tree."*

I had guessed that much. But with my cheek throbbing and much work to do, I was in no mood for humor.

Joining Gary to inspect the U-Haul, we saw that the front top of the van was smashed: the tree limb had caused a two-foot dent. After I got over the shock of the top corner being mashed in, my eyes gazed along the side of the van. I could see that it was no longer attached to the platform frame at all: the entire rear cab of the U-Haul had been ripped away from the floor of van.

Only adding to my misery was a growing number of spectators. Friends of mine, Chris and Billy, who had been following us in their car, were now standing alongside the van. Chris was laughing uncontrollably and I threatened him with bodily harm if he didn't stop. Billy just stood there, amazed. Others, my yet-to-be-met neighbors, also looked on, standing there in pajamas, slippers and early morning attire, startled or snickering.

Using straps, we managed to secure the van together well enough to drive back to the U-Haul rental office. As I entered the office that I had left only forty-five minutes earlier, the salesman asked what happened. Before I could respond, Gary repeated his catchphrase of that day, *"I think Ange hit a tree."*

A welt on my face and damage to the U-Haul as souvenirs, and a rather unceremonious introduction to my yet-to-be-met neighbors, the move was still a success. Three days later, I learned that the additional insurance rider that I had purchased – at the urging of Gary and Billy – for $6.10 had saved me $2,350 in total repairs. Then, a few days later, I was notified by the Village of Lancaster Police Department that I wouldn't have to pay for the damage to that tree, either; that limb was dead, they said, and had already been scheduled to be cut down.

I hung up the phone, sighed, then said to Pam, *"You won't believe this..."*

* * *

February 10 and it was 62 degrees outside. 62 in February in Buffalo! Call the Guinness Book of World Records!

My neighbor Wayne from across the street came over to see what I was doing on the porch. In addition to those who witnessed my U-Haul exploits, my wife and I have been extremely blessed with the neighbors we have met so far on Brandel Avenue, Wayne and his wife Karen included: welcoming and generous, easy to talk to. Time passes faster with good friends.

So does beer. Before we knew it, Wayne and I had drunk almost a half-case of beer. Wayne can drink like no one I knew to this point in my life. He would gulp down one of my treasured 6.0 alcohol content John Bradors, then look at the empty bottle and say, *"What the hell did you give me an empty bottle for?"* So I would get him another and it would disappear just as quick. In addition to drinking beer like a machine, Wayne's equally skilled at work. He's a carpenter and extremely fast, quality conscious, too.

Having just rehabbed this house and torn out all of the old windows from what used to be an enclosed sun porch, Wayne complimented me endlessly for my achievements on this house, especially the porch. We had bought this house as a fixer-upper and did just that. Old farmhouse style looks on the outside but deceivingly contemporary on the inside, our refurbished home has lots of open spaces.

Wayne said that he liked the outside, but he didn't think I knew much about painting interiors. The entire interior was painted white throughout, giving the house a brighter, bigger feel, ceilings seemingly higher, walls farther apart.

Wayne obviously didn't approve, but still conceded, *"You sure did wonders with this porch, it's a great place to drink beer... Speaking of beer, where the Hell is the beer that you promised me? This bottle is empty!"*

38 Brandel Avenue post-rehab.

After we finally finished rehabbing our house at 38 Brandel Avenue, Pam and I initiated a rule that no one - family included - would be allowed to smoke in our house. Pam and I don't smoke and we didn't want our girls exposed to second hand smoke. We now owned our own home and felt that we had the right to set the rules.

In addition to the health concerns of smoke, we had just finished an extensive, expensive, remodeling of the entire inside of the house and it still had that "new" smell to it. There was the fine scent of new carpets, drywall, paint, stained wood, and hardwood floor finish. At times I thought I could even still smell the charred sawdust of all the lumber I had cut with a skill-saw and power miter box. We wanted to maintain this "new" smell for as long as possible.

In order to honor all of the selfless contractors, family members and friends who had helped with the rehabbing of the house, we decided to throw a *"Thank You & Welcome"* party. So many people had been involved – each and all deserving thanks – that we knew they would not all fit into the house at the same time. We wanted people to come in and wander around, enjoy all we had done together. Our solution was to have a party on Saturday for friends and family, then a separate party on Sunday for contractors.

The first test of our "no smoking" policy came on Saturday. Two of the hardest workers were also the heaviest smokers. My father smoked more than two-and-a-half packs of cigarettes per day and my brother-in-law Kenny was a pipe smoker. After a short time in the house, hardly enough time to say *"Hello!"* to all of the guests, Dad and Kenny decided to go into the basement to *"inspect the pipes."* This was their code-speak for smoking.

Pam told me that she saw them heading to the back of the house where the basement entrance was, saying that they had *"that look in their eyes."*

I quickly caught up with them and asked where they were going. They gave their expected answer and I responded with, *"Sorry Dad, you know the rules. Kenny you know what I'm talking about..."*

So my father gave me that convincing smile of his, saying *"Just a quick one..."* Closing the basement door, I reiterated my concern as politely as possible. And Dad replied, stern as ever, *"I'm your father, damn it! I'm not smoking in the house, but in the basement... It won't smell!"*

"Dad, I said no."

He then tried to lay a guilt-trip on me – all of the work he put into the house, etc. etc. Standing firm, I politely told them both that this was our house and our rules stood. *"Besides,"* I added, *"Smoking is not good for you..."*

Annoyed but agreed, Dad demanded to know where they could smoke. I pointed toward the front of the house and said, *"Outside. On the porch."*

As they made their way to the bedroom to get their coats, everyone asked them where they were going. Dad answered as expected: *"Damn Angelo told me and Kenny that if we want to smoke we have to go smoke on the porch. Christ, it's freezing out there!"*

Everyone in earshot laughed at him, then slowly turned to me, as if to confirm that it was freezing outside. December in the Buffalo area is not fit for man or beast, and I was now banishing my father and brother-in-law into the frigid cold to inhale their smoke. Nonetheless, they went outside, onto the front porch, and the party continued.

After a few minutes, people inside began to move to the front windows to peer outside. Laughing, waving and gawking at these two grown men hunched over, huddled together in the crisp 15-degree air, trying to keep warm by clapping and rubbing their hands together. Seeing they were being spied, Kenny pretty much took it in stride but my father kept turning his back on the crowd, trying to ignore them. Soon enough, and well short of finishing their smokes, they were back at the front door begging to come in. We welcomed them back inside to a round of cheers.

Predictably, Pam and I took some jeering for why they were sent outside, into the Western New York winter. So I looked at my father and told him what he had told me countless times when I was growing up, but in a more loving tone, *"It's my house and you do what I say..."*

Hearing this, Dad played to the crowd a bit, howling how his own son had sent him outside to freeze, and the others laughed, making his whines somewhat successful.

Smiling, I then put the whole thing to rest. Casually, I informed him that I had been thinking about calling the cops and telling them to send a car. I'm a new homeowner, and the police should know that *"there are two strange men hanging out on my porch, looking in my windows..."*

* * *

Miko is the baby in our household now. I'm bottle-feeding her in my favorite porch chair, rocking her while she gives the nipple on the bottle a real working over. She doesn't just suck on the nipple: she attacks, trying to devour it.

She is the impatient one of our *"Darling Dago Daughters."* When things don't go as she plans, there is Hell to pay. Today is one of those days. It's chilly out and I'm trying to give her some fresh air, making sure to keep her bundled-up tightly. But she isn't interested in keeping warm and starts to squirm and kick and push away the blanket as she attacks her bottle.

Pam has said many times that this kid is extremely strong. I watch her push and fight the blanket, then me. Pam is right. I believe that this little one in my arms is going to be a strong athlete. I wonder what sort of athletic talent might be trapped inside of this little ball of muscle and intensity. If she is athletic in her years to come, I do know this: I would not want to be her competition.

* * *

I can hear him coming up the street even though I can't see him from where I sit on the porch. It's Mr. Softee. Actually, it's the Mr. Softee truck and the Mr. Softee music but it isn't the Mr. Softee we knew as kids. Someone must have bought the trucks and music and is trying to con the kids of today into thinking that this is what summer refreshment is all about.

I came to this conclusion when Danie and Miko, hearing the catchy music, ran to the curb and waved for the driver to stop, then yelled for me to please come and buy them something - Just like we did to our Dad when their age. He always would, for Tony, Janie and me, and all of our friends lucky enough to be around. A Dad now too, I joined my daughters at this pseudo Mr. Softee and opened my wallet. Turning and asking the girls what they wanted, they answered *"Cones with lots of colored sprinkles..."*

But when I asked the driver what size cones they had, he looked at me strangely. *"We don't have cones."*

I told the girls that they would have to have something else. They agreed. I then asked what kind of sundaes he had. *"We don't have sundaes."*

I asked about shakes. *"Sorry, don't have those, either."*

Disgusted, I asked what he did have and he pointed to a poster showing pictures of all kinds of frozen things with weird names; all some sort of Popsicle with prices out of this world.

Baffled, I leaned into the sliding window and looked into the truck. There were no ice cream machines, no cone dispensers and no milkshake makers. Amazed, I asked the driver, *"Hey, what happened to Mr. Softee?"*

"Who's Mr. Softee?"

* * *

Tonight was Trick or Treat. Pam dressed Danie and Miko up in their little costumes that they had designed themselves. I volunteered to take them around the neighborhood so they could go onto porches, ring doorbells, and beg for candy along with the hundreds of other kids that will assault our area tonight. I volunteered to do this because I hate to go to the door and dispense candy. Like my two little costumed daughters, I'd rather be on the receiving end.

Our neighbors know what being a kid on Halloween is all about and we got tons of candy. I watched the girls run up steps, ring doorbells and shout *"Trick or Treat!"* I saw them look into their bags through the eyeholes in their masks and smile at how much loot they had gathered. I heard them say *"Thank you!"* at each house. I also saw something else tonight, but it had nothing to do with masks, treats or doorbells. I saw my daughters hold each others' hands as they made their way from house to house, especially when they crossed the street. It was all about sisterhood, a bond between two little girls that I hope only grows as the years pass.

When we came home, I saw them dump the candy on the floor. And, when one of them realized that they had three Milky Way bars and the other only one, they tried to balance it out, exchanging treats so each had the same kind and quantity. It was a time for trading sweets, chewing, telling their mom about the scary monsters and that ugly witch they saw tonight. They even admitted how tired their arms were from carrying around these heavy bags of candy. Filling their mouths and laughing, our girls will sleep well tonight, after the sugar high ebbs of course.

Looking at Pam, I had to tell her.

"I love you for growing such great little people."

She just smiled.

* * *

Miko came out onto the porch and woke me up from one of my summer power naps, asking if it was okay if she walked up the street to Grandma Mike's house to play with the dogs. We called Pam's mom Grandma Mike because her real name is Elmera, and she was given the nickname Mike many years ago. Her dogs are Tina and Jasper. Tina is chestnut colored, hairy mutt, dumber than dumb, and as hyper as you can imagine. Jasper is a black Dachshund, smarter and more relaxed.

After about half an hour or so, I saw a sight straight out of a cartoon. Coming up the sidewalk toward our house was Miko, standing on a scooter with one end of a six-foot rope attached to the handle bar and the other attached to Jasper's collar. She was being pulled along by Jasper, but that wasn't the unusual part..

Jasper was being motivated to run, if there is such a thing with this breed of dog, by a carrot suspended in front of him. And Miko was holding a stick, with that carrot dangling just out of Jasper's reach. The dog was running with all its might to grab it; but the faster he ran, the faster Miko went. The smile on her face was as big as the Grand Canyon.

Awed, I waved and shouted, *"Way to go Miko!"*

Life imitates art when you least expect it.

* * *

Pam and I threw an end of season pool party for the softball team that I coached and Miko played on. Call me biased, but she was my player extraordinaire... The yard was full of twelve-year-old cackling, laughing, screaming, and giggling girls. We had pizza and wings because, at this point in the summer, most people have had their fill of hot dogs on the grill. We even had a cake to celebrate their victories.

Pam and I watched from the deck as the girls jumped in the pool, climbed up the ladder, turned around and jumped back in, over and over, again and again. I got tired just watching them. Later, I went into the house and grabbed two fists full of change, returned to the side of the pool and tossed it all in. Alternating, the girls leapt off the deck, into the water, retrieving all the coins they could scour and snatch from the bottom. This finally tired them out and Pam rented a movie for them to watch: *"A League of Their Own"* about the first women's pro baseball league.

The girls came in, feasted on popcorn and pop, watching the movie in silence. Pam and I cleaned up, then went outside to sit on the porch. With the windows open we heard nothing but the sound of the voices on the TV. I thought to myself how important this time was and is for these girls. They were just part of something special, an entire twelve-game season (with only three losses) plus playoffs. I wondered if they saw themselves as the individual characters in that movie or as something far greater: a team. I like to think of every team that I coach as special, each one unique; not because of me or Pam, who always kept score, though... It was because of the girls that were on it: exciting, respectful, talented, fun-loving young ladies.

From the porch, we listened until the movie ended. There was no laughing and giggling. Just a short silence, and then they all seemed to say as one *"That was good."*

Yes it was... I thought to myself, *That was good.*

* * *

I'm in my office in school, putting folders full of papers into one of my filing cabinets. I'm usually so busy with prep work for my classes that I rarely spend any time in here. About the only thing I do in here each day is put my jacket on the back of my chair, unlock the desk drawer and make a pot of coffee.

I look up from the drawers full of folders and, there in front of me, is the picture of Danie and Miko in their Lancaster High School volleyball team jerseys. The picture was taken three years ago. Pam asked the girls on that day to put their jerseys on because she wanted to take their picture in the driveway, next to the porch. The porch is the place for pictures in my family. They whined heavily about having to do it, and I sort of yelled at them. *"Damn it! Just do it!"*

Now, as I look at that picture of them, their arms over each other's shoulders, standing close, I see two sisters connected by more than their last name, team colors and jerseys. I see the same two girls that I remember holding hands on trick or treat night many years ago as they crossed the street to gather more loot. I see in their eyes the mischief of many plots against Pam and me, when they wanted to play us against each other for the sake of their common goal, good or otherwise.

I flash back to when they made us breakfast and presented us with a bill from *"Moots and Poots Diner"* (just two of the assorted nicknames they have had over the years...). I recall them rooting and cheering for each other in sports; even when one was playing and the other wasn't. I also dwell on the fact that, more than likely, they will never wear the same team colors again. This in itself makes me blue.

Her senior year, Danie's wish was that Miko would make the varsity volleyball team so they could play side by side in the back row. Her wish came true that year, and they were as stalwart a defense as ever assembled. No ball hit the floor when they were on the court together.

I see something that this photo doesn't show. I see two darling daughters that have proven over the years that they will help each other to be strong, to encourage each other as they move through their lives. Together, they helped their school team win the division championship. Trophies in hand, they were officially winners.

For me though, staring at that picture, my throat lumps up as I whisper, *"If you only knew what winners you have always been in my eyes."*

* * *

From my porch I heard Brian, our young neighbor from next door, call to his mom, *"Mom please cross me!"* He's still in his early years of elementary school and isn't allowed to cross the street without one of his parents coming to the curb to watch for approaching cars. When I heard him yell this, and watching him wait for his mom to escort him across the street, it brought back memories of when Danie and Miko were very young and they did the exact same thing.

"Papa will you cross me?"

Many times I'd have to leave my comfort zone on the porch to cross them so they could go play with their little friends that lived on the street perpendicular to ours. I can remember how, as I walked them across the street, their small hands would grab my whole index finger and hold on to it so tightly. It was almost as if they were getting an extra sense of security by doing that. And, when we got to the other side of the street, only then would they let go of my finger. And I would always assure them that I would be there to cross them back by saying, *"You just yell for me and I'll be here."*

As each year passed, their trips to their friend's house continued, but my trips across the street became shorter and shorter. It got to the point where I would just lean forward in my chair on the porch, look up and down the street, then tell them that it was safe to cross. They no longer need to be crossed, no need to hold my index finger anymore. These days, it's only when they are backing the car out of the driveway do they ask, *"Papa will you watch me back out?"*

I do and, as they back out, they smile, wave, then drive off.

* * *

It's about 10:30 at night and so hauntingly quiet. Pam and Miko are in New Orleans for the Junior Olympic Volleyball Nationals, and Danie is off somewhere with her friends. I'm alone, on the porch, unusually unsettled.

Trying to relax, I lean back, then just listen. There is sound, it's not so quiet after all, crickets directly beneath me, under the porch floor, rubbing their wings, ringing of song.

That's a sound that we don't hear much around here. I wonder if we don't hear the crickets because the weather conditions have not been right or due to the recent boom in development of housing in our area, scaring them off. I seem to remember hearing crickets all of the time when I was growing up in South Buffalo.

Were they always here? Am I now too busy to stop and listen?

For my sake, I hope it is over-development.

* * *

July 4th... For the first time in many years, the parade is going to pass down our street, right in front of our house. Our porch will be an excellent place to gather and watch the parade, as it is just twenty feet from the curb.

Lancaster always has a parade. In the downtown area, they have rides for the kids, an art show, a bunch of booths and beer tent. This year is somewhat special in that my brother Tony is in town from Missouri. It is also sort of strange because Pam and Miko are still in New Orleans with Miko's volleyball team competing in the Junior Olympic nationals and will return later today, in time to eat and watch the fireworks show.

My parents, mother-in-law, brother Tony, sister Janie and her husband Kenny will be here along with a bunch of other friends and relatives. This year I invited my good friend Russ, his wife Maria and son Michael. Russ is my age but he was born in Italy, or as my father would say *"The Old Country."* He and Dad both speak Italian pretty well, have a gift for conversation, and are always full of tales of Italy, its culture, people, and much of it in Italian using phrases from *"The Old Country."*

Listening to them always gets me thinking how wonderful it would have been if my parents had taught us a little Italian when we were growing up. It is such a pretty language to listen to. My daughters have asked me many times why I can't speak Italian and I feel bad that I couldn't pass the language along to them. It gives me a feeling of loss.

As the generations pass, so do the native languages and many of the customs of those before. This is a real shame because those that I was surrounded by and always enjoyed when I was young will not pass onto my children, or theirs'. More than just language and culture, this is made all the more difficult because times are so much different today. Families live farther apart and we are all so busy, always caught-up in one thing another, or so it seems.

Even though Pam and I call our daughters the *"Darling Dago Daughters,"* I regret the Italian customs and traditions that they will never have the joy of experiencing in their lifetime.

* * *

I walked across the street to meet the new neighbors who were sitting on their front porch: a mom and her two sons. They have been here for a while, but I just never had the chance to say hello, to formally welcome them to the neighborhood. One of the boys is Danie's age, and the other is Miko's. They are somewhat of a rarity in the neighborhood, though, as they have an African-American father and a Caucasian mother.

The older son is an excellent basketball player. He has come over to our driveway many times to shoot around with the girls, who are pretty good shots, themselves. He really impressed them with his talent for the game. One day he invited Danie over to their yard to play a pick-up game with his father, who doesn't live with them. Well, Danie didn't need to be asked twice, she is a real basketball fanatic, and when she got home she couldn't wait to tell me that she had a ball playing with them.

While I was talking to the boys' mom today - when we finally, officially, met - I couldn't resist telling her about Danie's comments after the pick-up game. When

Danie told me about how much fun she had, she had also said, *"Papa, when the boys told me that their dad was big and tall and black, I knew that he would be a good basket-ball player... He was awesome!"* Our new neighbor roared with delight after hearing this.

Once again, my *"Darling Dago Daughters"* have shown me that the innocence of youth is a priceless com-modity.

* * *

The phone rang at about 8:00 p.m. The voice on the line said that my father and mother's house on Sheffield Avenue was on fire. I asked if they were hurt and the caller said that they weren't but I should get there as soon as pos-sible. My mother was asking for me. I hung-up the phone, told Pam what I just heard and, as we made our way to the car, I asked her not to say a word to me about my driving from this point forward. I was about to break several rules of the road. The normal twenty-minute drive to South Buf-falo took me eight minutes.

As I turned onto Sheffield Avenue, the police turned me away and back onto McKinley Parkway, so we parked the car and rushed toward the house. There were fire trucks and red flashing lights everywhere. The crowd that had already gathered was extremely large - this was the biggest thing to hit Sheffield Avenue in decades! Running and pushing, the neighbor two houses away shouted from her porch to us that my mother was there with them and my father was with the firemen.

"With the firemen?"

The fire was caused by high winds blowing a tree over onto the power lines in front of our house. The line pulled from the utility pole and shorted itself out on the power panel in the basement of Mom and Dad's home. My parents were at the bowling alley at the time but my cousin happened to be walking by and saw bright red coming from the basement window. She called the fire department, then my parents at the bowling alley; the entire basement was ablaze by then and moving upward quickly.

Mom and Dad arrived just when the fire department did. Humorously, Dad actually unlocked the side door for the firefighters so that they wouldn't have to break it down. He succeeded, they went in, then opened windows and the front door to evacuate the smoke. Luckily, they managed to put out the fire just as it was breaching through the living room floor, catching the carpet and pad on fire. The total damage was a little over $19,000. It could have been much worse.

As the action was winding down - interviews being given to the TV and newspaper reporters – I surveyed the surreal scene. I could peer through the charred hole in the living room floor right into the basement. There was water everywhere and the entire house reeked of smoke. And then I noticed that all of the furniture in the living room had been carried out through the front door and placed neatly on the astroturf-covered porch deck. Of all of the windows that were used to evacuate the smoke, not one was broken; all were opened as if someone was trying to let fresh air in rather than harsh smoke out.

I sought out the fire chief in charge and thanked him and his crew for the quick action. I then asked him why no windows were broken and no furniture destroyed, but so carefully, deliberately, carried outside of the house and placed safe from harm?

Looking around as if someone might overhear him, the fire chief said, *"Very seldom do we worry about doors, windows and furniture. Our job is to get people out of the house first, then to put out the fire as quickly as possible. When we pulled up at the same time as your father and he offered to open the door, I felt that we had a head start. When I walked into the living room as the other guys went into the basement, I saw that this house was something spe-cial to this man. I told the guys to do what I felt we should do."* Breaking a smile, he added, *" I also didn't want to have your dad worry about broken glass on his astroturf carpet on the porch."*

Grateful, smiling and shaking my head, I thanked the fire chief again, then turned to find Mom. She was still on the neighbor's front porch, crying uncontrollably by now. Pam was beside her, trying to comfort her. As I approached Mom, she was saying over and over again, *"My house, my house, oh Angelo, my house..."*

I tried to console her, but she wasn't even hearing my voice. The porch was filling with well-wishers, offers of food and a place to sleep tonight. She was still hysterical, though, getting worse, so I grabbed her by the shoulders and forced her to look into my eyes. *"Mom, get a hold of yourself! I'm taking you into the Kathy's house right now."* And I did just that.

In Kathy's house, we managed to settle Mom down somewhat. And then a neighbor yelled at me for yelling at my mother. After a while, I apologized to my mother and assured her that I didn't mean to act like that; tonight has been a tough one for everyone. Afterward, more settled now, we just sat there, talking quietly, reflecting. Someone asked me about the damage to the house.

Then, out of nowhere, Mom looked up at me and said, *"Mister, don't you ever talk to me like that again. I'm still your mother."* And, in almost the same motion, she looked down into her tissue, picked her head back up, then pleaded to me, *"Angelo, will you and your friends make the house nice again?"*

And I took Mom's hands, looked into her eyes, and assured her that we would do just that.

* * *

It was pretty early in the morning when I stopped by Mom and Dad's house, but both of them were already up. I was on my way to give a customer an estimate on some ceramic tile, not too far from Sheffield Avenue. So Dad and I sat on the porch drinking coffee, and Mom, her tea. We were all in our favorite chairs as we talked; me with my feet up on the railings as I had done for years, back to when I was growing up in this house. Dad no longer yells and screams at me to take my feet down; I believe he has mellowed somewhat. The railings on his porch are nice and wide. They easily accommodate a coffee cup of any size, a can or bottle of beer or pop, a small plate and, in Dad's case: an ashtray.

Dad has been a heavy smoker since he was seventeen years old. Now in his seventies, we are all sure that his lungs are pretty much devastated by smoke and nicotine. One look at the two fingers that he uses to hold his cigarettes shows what they have done to him. I remember early mornings in this house when I was growing up, and the four sounds that were most distinct. The first was his alarm clock; the second the sound of his Zippo lighter being opened and ignited almost simultaneously; the third the exhale after the first long drag of the day; the last was the sound of Dad coughing...

For years we have asked, told, begged for him to stop, not only for his sake, but Mom's. She has been breathing his second-hand smoke for decades. The ceilings in the house are yellow with smoke stains. Nonetheless, his response is always the same, *"Listen, I've been smoking since I was seventeen years old. You don't know how hard it is to stop."*

Today, as we sit and talk on their porch, my eyes happen to catch a blue can sitting on the floor near the front post and Dad's chair. It is a Maxwell House coffee can. I motion in the direction of the can and ask Dad what it's for. Mom chimes-in before he can answer, *"Go look, Angelo, it's his new ashtray."*

I get up, walk over to the can and look inside. Countless butts, bent and brown, fill the can. *"What the Hell's the matter with you? Are you crazy or something?"*

Defensive about smoking as ever, Dad answers that they are not all from today but from a few days. He has a smirk on his face when he says this, and we get into another argument about his smoking. I know it will end with the same old quote about smoking since he was seventeen.

This time, though, Mom interrupts us with, *"Angelo, I told him but he won't listen to me..."*

So I ask if he cares about Mom's health and Dad mumbles something about all that secondhand smoke stuff being *"BS."* Trying to end this useless debate, I offer that, even though he doesn't care about his health, his family does. Returning to my seat, Dad remarks coldly, *"Look, if you don't like it, you don't have to come here and put up with it."*

Enough said, I grab my coffee cup off of the railing, go into the house and put it in the kitchen sink. Returning to the porch, I give Mom a little hug and kiss and tell her goodbye.

As I leave, Dad wonders, *"Where are you going?"*

"I'm taking your advice Dad. I don't have to put up with you or your cigarettes. When you get rid of that can, I'll come back..."

* * *

Danie and Miko were warming up for their respective softball games for the town's recreational league called *"Ponytails."* Danie plays outfield on the 16's team while Miko pitches on the 14's team: the team that I coach. They were positioned on the lawn in front of the porch about thirty feet apart and I was sitting in my usual spot. I was supposed to be just watching, but I couldn't help myself. I offered a little coaching regarding Miko's pitching.

This went on for the better part of half an hour. They were pitching, catching, and making small talk about something or another. In all of the sports that she played, Danie would always ask how she was doing or seek extra help from whoever the coach might be. Miko, on the other hand, doesn't tolerate or request critiques. This doesn't mean that she isn't coach-able; for the most part she does things very well and she knows it, but never in a cocky or egotistical way.

As I watched them, I noticed that they were wearing the grass down in the areas where they were standing. I told them that they should change their locations in order to *"take it easy on the grass."*

Danie, always one to speak her mind, told me to *"quit worrying about the dumb old grass."*

It took me about ten seconds to lose my composure and I went into a tirade about when I was growing up.

When we were young on Sheffield Avenue and brought friends over to our yard to play, my father would always howl how we were ruining *"his grass."* According to Dad, we would *"make it brown and kill it."* When his warnings failed – we rarely gave-in and left – he would throw us out of the yard, obscenities following our every step.

This time, though, I had hardly finished my tirade to my girls before realizing, then saying, *"My God, I sound just like Dad..."*

I love my father and have always tried to be like him in many ways. But this was not on the list. At that point I did something that he never did.

I apologized.

* * *

I figured that today I would go home for lunch and see how my father was coming along with stripping the shingles from the house. Dad and Uncle Frank said that they would help strip the shingles and clapboards from the house so we could have vinyl siding put on. They were masters of the ladder routine, having been roofers when they were growing up in Geneva, New York. Dad always told the story of Uncle Frank falling off of a church steeple in the wintertime. Fortunately, he landed in a five-foot snow bank near the base of the church, got up, dusted himself off, then walked over to the ladder and went back up onto the roof.

As I pulled down the street, I saw my father sitting on the edge of the porch eating his lunch: a pepperoni and egg sandwich. It was sublime. Here was this small man sitting on the massive porch of a massive house, chewing, smiling, saying, *"Don't you have anything better to do than ride around in a car all day?"*

I just so happened to have a camera and I snapped a picture of him sitting there. I really didn't need a picture to remember this scene in time, as it was already etched in my mind. I think it was because, unconsciously, I wanted to remember what he looked like when he was healthy and able to do things like this.

In years to come, his good health might only be a memory to both of us. Someday I won't be able to ask him to do physical favors for me like I do now. And, when that day comes, I will just have to look around this house and recall how much of him and his expertise went into what has been a wonderful home for Pam and me to raise our girls.

Sitting there, waiting as he finished his lunch, we talked for a while longer. And then I told my father that it was time for me to ride around in the car again.

* * *

Preparing the garage for winter today, putting things in their seasonal storage spaces, I had to make room for the Corvette, putting her to sleep over in the corner. This is a routine of mine every October.

While moving things, I came across the citronella candles on the floor and put them on the wire storage rack. Doing this, for some reason, I lifted one of the candles to my nose and took a long, deep inhale.

For a split second I was transported back to the front porch, mid-July and the smell of citronella wafting up from under my rocker, mosquitoes sucking my sweet Italian blood... All brought back this one smell.

Like me with walnuts and Uncle Joey, a good friend of ours can recall memorable places or events that happened to her just by eating certain things.

It's so cute how she looks at her husband and says, *"This muffin reminds me of... Do you remember?"*

She always gets upset when he says, *"No, I don't."*

* * *

In the high school where I teach, I am a co-adviser to the Technology Club. This is an after-school club that meets once a week, is open to any student in the school, and has no membership requirements. It is just a group of students who show up on Thursdays on a regular basis with the common goal of doing projects for the school or themselves.

This year we were struggling for a mass production project idea. After spending many splendid hours this past summer on my porch swing, I suggested that we use the idea of a porch swing for our project. There was a bit of selfishness behind my suggestion: my porch swing had seen better days. It has served us for almost sixteen years but was now starting to come apart. After little discussion, it was decided that we would make porch swings and sell them.

Before the club met the next week, I carefully disassembled the swing that had hung from my porch ceiling for those many years and, within a few hours, I had traced all of the wooden pieces onto cardboard in order to make templates and patterns. My swing was made out of poplar but the new ones would be made out of red oak: the wood that most old-fashioned swings were usually made of. In the meantime, the students had been busy taking preorders and, after talking it over, it was decided that nine swings would be our mass production project for that year.

Gearing-up for full production, I started pulling the necessary lumber for the seats and back slats. I tried to find wood that was somewhat benign in its natural characteristics – in other words, lacking knots and discoloration. The wood grain pattern should also be tight. Since the under-supports would be hidden - their function being only structural strength for the seats and back slats - the oak used for this specific part of each swing wouldn't have to be superior in appearance. But the rest – all that is on top and exposed – would have to be the best we could find. We looked over the wood carefully, meticulously, especially for the arms, trying to select a nice grain pattern to really accent the rest of the swing. The students were a bit impatient with my fussiness over the wood we were to use, bored with inspecting oak and grains, all too eager to start building, but I told them it would be worth it in the end.

Once accomplished, our materials at last ready for production, we then carefully traced the patterns for the best aesthetic appeal. The nine swings slowly emerged, teacher and students working together, creating truly beautiful porch swings for the community. Upon completing the project, we then discussed and evaluated what we had made, and all we had learned. We sold some of the swings, gave one to a scholarship auction in the name of an excellent teacher in our school who had recently passed away, and I bought one.

Like they had been about building, I was now eager to hang my new porch swing from its anchor eyebolts protruding from my porch ceiling. After doing so, I then stood back to admire what a fine piece of woodwork we had produced, noticing the grain pattern in the arms and the new glossy finish that graced the oak. I then sat in it, pushed myself off as I always did, and noticed that there was a different feel to the arms. They were not rough and weathered like the arms on my old poplar swing. The slats under my butt felt almost too smooth, giving me the feeling that I might slip off during the back-swing motion. The only thing that felt the same was the chain.

Though I had replaced my swing, I had reused the old chain – more functional than sentimental, I suppose. And, in doing so, I noticed that the familiar sounds that the chains had made as the swing went back and forth were not the same. Up until now, on the old swing, the chains seemed to *"groan"* in the forward motion and *"sigh"* in the backward motion. The groan and sigh were now gone, replaced by a rather annoying squeaking sound. So annoying that, after a few minutes of swinging, I rose to retrieve the

WD-40 from the garage. I sprayed the heck out of the links, from where they hung from the anchor eyebolts to where they attached to the swing. And then I sat back down. Pushing myself off again, I swung some more, relieved to hear nothing at all, not a sound.

After a few minutes more of trying to get used to the fit and feel of my swing, something else started to bother me. Even though we had made a new and improved version of an American porch fixture, and in the process replaced the worn and weathered swing on my porch, we could never replace its soul. The groan and the sigh were gone, and only years of use, sitting and swinging, might bring them back.

Author's Aunt Mary and Uncle John's home at
660 McKinley Parkway.

I remember my Aunt Mary, her big South Buffalo home, and little Chico the dog, his paws propping him up on the railing, barking at passersby. A sweltering day on a grand old porch, perfect people watching along McKinley Parkway. Aunt Mary's porch was meant for sitting and watching: on the corner, two streets in full view, activity all around.

I thought Aunt Mary would be here forever, always on her porch when the weather was nice. When I was young, she was indestructible, moving the furniture in her living room so my brother Tony and I could play tackle football. She played too, a great blocker, and bruiser. As she said, she had *"great pads"* – meaning her big boobs – Just the person to lead-block on a goal-line stand.

No one is indestructible, even Aunt Mary, and she died of what the doctors said was a "peaceful heart attack" a few years ago. I was in my late forties then, and wondered what could be so peaceful about my favorite aunt dying? Only now do I fully understand...

Danie and Miko had called her on the phone earlier that morning to say *"Hi!"* and get well soon. Pam and I had visited her in the hospital that afternoon and she seemed fine. As we got ready to leave, Pam and I both kissed her goodbye, and Aunt Mary made sure to tell me to kiss the girls for her. Looking back, I wonder if she was waiting, maybe holding out, for us to visit before she finally passed. In hindsight, peacefully...

When the weather is nice, each time I pass by her old house on the corner of McKinley and Como, I see her there in spirit. Chico too, propped and barking. She has her apron on and is sitting in her old blue metal chair, leaning forward and waving and smiling at me like she did so many times when I drove by in my Corvair. I always tooted the horn for her.

I would trade everything I own to have her lead the charge, over the goal-line, into the imaginary end-zone in her home. Raising both arms into the air once more, 1 can hear her yelling *"Touchdown!"*

* * *

Aunt Mary and Uncle John are no longer alive but their wonderful house on McKinley Parkway is still in the family. After Uncle John passed, and planning for her own, Aunt Mary set up a trust that turned the house over to my sister Janie, my brother Tony and me. We now rent both the upper and lower apartments, keeping that wonderful old home full. Such a place shouldn't be empty nor fall into the hands of strangers.

Now landlords, we provide a nice place to live and expect the tenants to keep the property maintained, meaning cutting the lawn and shoveling the snow. This is a real point of contention, though. The tenants' version of cutting the grass is to not cut it at all, while shoveling snow to them is beating a footpath to the driveway, just wide enough for a person to walk through. Clearing the snow from the driveway is done with their car tires, packing it down, or plowing with their front or rear bumpers if a storm just hit. Perhaps due to the snow, or the tenants' universal refusal to shovel whatsoever, the front doors of the house are rarely used, and both the upper and lower porches bear the load of snow all winter long.

The snowfall over the past week would put all of us to the test. It began snowing on Christmas Eve and didn't let up until South Buffalo was buried under seven feet of white. In Lancaster, we accumulated a mere six and one-half feet. Lucky us! My brother was in town from Missouri and supposed to fly out Christmas evening, but he was snowed-in until New Year's Day. Even by Buffalo standards, this was an outrageous storm. Just like during the Blizzard of '77 - the storm that brought Buffalo to the forefront of winter infamy - the people of the city and outlying areas pulled together to help each other in any way they could. Acts of heroism and good neighborliness abounds in Buffalo during blizzards. Other than that, the only fortunate feature of this most recent ordeal (and not for the students) was that the storm hit while all of the schools were on break for the holidays.

A driving ban was in place for several days, and when it was finally lifted, I was at last allowed to get to South Buffalo. My mission twofold: safely arrive at the rental property at 660 McKinley Parkway, then shovel the mountains of snow off the upper porch deck. For a few too many years, the roof has been sagging under its own weight: right down the middle from left to right when viewed head-on. This is due to Uncle John; he removed the center support post for the upper deck when the house was being covered with aluminum siding and never bothered replacing it. After we took ownership of the house, we got estimates on correcting the problem from a handful of contractors, with prices ranging from $3,500 to over $11,000. After some discussion, my sister and I decided to try to hold off until the house was sold. We hoped its new owners would appreciate a price-break for the work that needed to be done; more so, they could repair it to their own liking. It was a bit unsightly, but certainly not unsafe. Until this snowstorm, that is...

I wound up parking half a block away because the side streets were still impassible. Mounds of snow were everywhere. Only the main artery streets had been cleared, all of the side streets would have to wait. South Buffalo looked like the lunar landscape, there was no activity anywhere; yet another reminder of yet another blizzard, when our Mayor instructed us *"Get a 6-pack and stay inside..."*

I was wearing over-the-knee fireman boots, winter clothing for extreme situations just like this, and carrying two shovels. I knew enough to pack some provisions in case I got stranded: Reese's Peanut Butter Cups, the cell phone, a bottle of LaBatts Blue beer and some Twizzlers licorice. As I approached the house, I was immediately aware of the job I had before me. Everything was literally buried. The porch steps were nonexistent and the side door was a mirage of white.

I managed to make it into the side door, into the upstairs apartment, and to the front windows overlooking the upper porch deck. As I looked at the snow – almost neck-high, compressed and compacted from melting and evaporating by the prevailing winds out of the west – I felt helpless; unnerved by what lay ahead. I asked myself *"Am I & *%# crazy?!"*

Pushing open the porch door, I commenced shoveling. Due to its wet weight and my inability to reach the railing in order to dump it over, I could only toss each shovel-full in front of me, piling it higher and higher, until I finally cleared a path to the railing. At that moment, the thirteen-foot wide by twenty-two foot long porch seemed to be as large as an aircraft carrier.

Just then, another concern filled my mind: Would the added weight of my body send the porch decking crumbling to the floor below? I knew that this roof was unsupported – *Thanks Uncle John!* – I could go crashing downward, falling far and hard, tons of snow joining me below, at any moment. So I retrieved the cell phone from just inside the door and slipped it into my pocket. Should I become the victim of an avalanche, I had better be able to call for help...

Continuing, I attacked the snow at first, mostly out of frustration. After a while, my winter instincts took over and I started to pace myself. All too soon, my arms grew tired and my back ached. Living in this area you learn how to properly shovel snow: how to use your legs, knees, arms and back in a harmony that won't give you a heart attack. That logic seemed to be useless in this instance, though; this wasn't shoveling by its normal definition, more like moving a mountain.

After shoveling, lifting and groaning for almost five hours, I was finally done. I could at last stop and see just how foolish I had been all along. My toes and fingers had almost no feeling to them, in spite of the fact that I was dressed like an Eskimo.

"I am & *%# crazy!"

Finished, I let out a yell and punched the air. I had conquered all this snow. I put the edge of the shovel on the porch deck, both palms over the handle, rested my chin atop, and gazed off at the gray sky. I believe that this is where the souls of Aunt Mary, Uncle John and Grandpa Frank now reside.

I managed a smile.

The time spent doing this job allowed me to ponder some of the memories of this porch and this apartment. We lived here – above Aunt Mary, Uncle John and Grandpa Frank – for a few years after moving from the East Side of Buffalo. I was two years old and we stayed here until our move to 193 Sheffield Avenue when I was five.

I looked at the wrought iron railings and realized that, based on today's building codes, these railings would be illegal. The space between the bars are wide enough for a small child to pass through, crawl to the edge and fall off. That didn't seem to concern my parents or grandparents back then. Even so, they never let me stay on the porch by myself as a baby, anyway.

I remember watching Dad go over the railing one day, lifting one leg at a time, to clean the leaves out of the gutter. I thought he was really brave. I always wanted to do that, too: to step over the railing when I got older, to prove my bravery. But we moved before I was able to do so.

Mom would spread the blanket on the deck, which is galvanized tin covering the wooden boards beneath. She would bring us onto the porch but always stayed with us, making sure that we were on that blanket because she feared we might get cut on the tin seams.

I remember eating out on this porch, only once. Dad set up the small, metal card table with matching metal folding chairs. Mom seemed annoyed by the whole process of bringing food out on the porch. Living here for only three years was never enough time to enjoy all this porch could have offered-up as we grew older.

I walked over to the railing overlooking the stairs that led to the wooden porch floor downstairs. There and then I realized that the porch beneath me was where my most cherished memories of 660 McKinley Parkway had taken place, albeit after we moved out of this house.

Aunt Mary and Uncle John lived here; they sat on that porch for another forty years. We were here constantly. They were like second parents to us, and we were the children they never had.

* * *

I decided that today would be a good day to scrub
and power-wash the mahogany porch floor. It's only 6:00
a.m. and already seventy-two degrees; the floor will dry
quickly. I can re-coat the surface with oil-based finish in
just a few days. This is not a job that I enjoy, nor one that I
look forward to, but I know that when I'm done and the
new finish is applied in a few days, the porch floor will be a
thing of beauty once again. I look at it the same way that I
do when I wash, strip and wax my car.

After gathering all of the items that I'll need, I apply the stripper chemical to the floor with a medium nap
roller. This penetrates the old finish and allows me to blast
it away with the power-washer. After applying it, I allow it
to soak in about fifteen minutes then attack it with a plastic
bristled broom prior to power-washing. This is a lot of
physical work and takes me about four hours to complete.
Eventually, my hands grow numb from the pulsing action
of the power-washer.

After the washing is complete, I take a rubber
bladed squeegee and remove all of the excess water from
the floor. I notice, just as I do every time that I do this job,
a small puddle of water always remains in one particular
section of the floor. It is the section where a few boards
attached to one another sit just beneath the surface and
aren't level with the boards adjacent to them. The squee-

gee passes right over the water, leaving that annoying puddle. I smile and say in a low voice, *"Uncle John...."*

Before we installed this floor, we had to add cross-bracing between the floor joist members. I was very particular in the way we did this, ever attentive to (Pam says anal about) detail. Well, this particular spot is the one that Uncle John worked on... We had to put the nails in at a diagonal to some of the boards, allowing them to pull both boards together. It is a difficult nailing procedure, and Uncle John kept pounding, cursing, then pulling out the same nail countless times. I told him to just throw the nail away and get another one but - as he had proved in finding me the best but cheapest spindles and railings for this same porch – Uncle John was always very frugal. A new nail wouldn't make the task any easier, and only prolong the inevitable.

To his credit, Uncle John was a very good craftsman who could do just about anything with his hands, but nailing like this, on a diagonal, was his Mt. Everest. After beating the nail into place somewhat successfully, he called me over to check the alignment of the top surface of the bracing to the joists. I did and it was low, just as I thought it might be.

After seeing this, Uncle John looked up at me and asked, *"Angelo, does it matter? No one will ever see it..."*

Appearing to think about it, feigning approval really, I said, *"Uncle John, that's close enough. You're right. No one will ever see it."*

Years later, I do see it. I see it every time it rains; the snow melts; I wash it... I even see it every time I walk over it, wet or dry. More so, I remember how Uncle John gave up every Sunday - his only day off from working at his grocery – for over five months to help me make this house into a home.

There are many things that he did while working on this house that people have forgotten, and no one ever saw. This is one thing that I will always see, though. And, every time I do, I see Uncle John, on his knees, resting his hands on his hammer, looking up at me.

"Thank God it didn't matter."

* * *

Today was an enigma. Filled with both heavy grief and great joy, I have had few days that compare to this one.

Pam's younger brother Michael, who lived in Virginia, passed away a few days ago at the age of only forty-two. He had a brain aneurysm in his sleep and never woke.

Needless to say, losing Michael was most unexpected. No one can nor should predict another's passing, but Pop had been diagnosed with lung cancer only last year, and as Pam put it, *"Everyone thought that the next funeral would be his."* Not Michael's, surely not him, so young, so quickly.

His body was brought back home to Lancaster for the funeral, and all of the family and close friends gathered on Grandma Mike and Pop's front porch after the funeral breakfast. The purpose of the gathering was to sit, relax and console. All too soon, it turned into a mass of remembrance: of Michael's life and his time here, at 37 Erie Street, growing up in our neighborhood.

Pam's family is huge, with her, a younger sister, and six younger brothers, five minus Michael now... Combined with Grandma Mike's and Pop's memories, they have volumes of stories about him. The somber mood slowly grew into a contest, with relatives and friends trying to offer the funniest stories; one leading to another, hilarious memories of Michael triggering even more, tears of sadness overwhelmed by those of joy. We were all laughing so hard that we were coughing, bellies aching, roaring.

Amongst the most memorable stories were those when Michael got into "no good" – as his mother always said. She had a way of finding out, though, one so unusual yet effective that it never failed. She would question him while he slept. Tucked in his bed, snoozing seemingly in peace, Michael would confess everything, providing all the answers his mother was seeking. Then, later, when she confronted him about whatever "no good" he'd done, Michael could never figure out how she knew.

And then there was the time when he asked to use the family car and was refused. So he went out to the car, then caved-in the windshield with a crowbar. Certainly no poster-child for good behavior, Michael always had a smile on his face and a knack for making everyone laugh. He will always be remembered as a real charmer, no matter how much "no good" he got into. Everyone agreed that he was a good husband and good father to his daughter, now in her teens; perhaps the two highest compliments available.

I couldn't offer any stories about Michael's youth, since I didn't know him back then, so I listened intently, taking in what the others said, then laughing just as hard as them, like I'd known him all my life. I felt privileged to have married into this family. Michael was and is blessed.

There's Pop, sitting in his favorite chair on the porch, surrounded by his "numerous progeny" – as he would often refer to them. And there's Pam's mom, Grandma Mike to Danie and Miko, sitting in her designated seat. Both her and Pop seem to be doing extremely well, considering the cause of this particular congregation.

Stories shared, tears shed, it was soon time for everyone to leave. Paying our final condolences with handshakes, hugs and kisses, we all said the fondest of farewells.

It was then that a scene from one of Jack Kerouac's books came to mind. I can't remember which, but that moment inspired Jack's words: A bunch of "Beatniks" (a term that Kerouac coined but seldom used) are leaving a restaurant after eating, talking, enjoying one another's company, and how the narrator mentions that indescribable feeling... That same feeling I had right then, watching so much family and many friends leaving, stepping off the porch. It occurred to him just then, as they all got up, pushed their chairs under the table, and parted ways. This moment will never be repeated again.

In the book, I believe Jack Kerouac called it an enigma. Today was no different, but utterly unique. What took place on this porch was a true American enigma.

* * *

It's Junior Prom night. Danie has been spending what seems like the entire day getting ready. She told me to keep an eye out for her friend Marc who would be coming over for me to take pictures of them – even though they were not going together but with different dates.

When Marc arrived, I took a few pictures of them together on the porch, right where many other photos of the girls have taken place over the years. We also took some out on the lawn and I even allowed Marc to wear his base-ball hat for one of the pictures. The hat was his trademark; he wore it everywhere. Looking at them standing together, side by side in the picture, one would want to chuckle. Danie is a diminutive 4'9" while Marc towers about a foot taller. In his suit, he seemed twice her size.

Having taken enough pictures at our house, Pam suggested that we walk up the street and take some with Grandma Mike and Pop. By then, Pop was almost bedrid-den with cancer. He wanted his last days to be spent at home rather than in a hospital, and Hospice granted this last wish.

Pam's mother suggested that we come into the house for the picture because Pop was so weak. We were preparing to do just that, and she explained to Pop what was going to happen. And then I heard him say, in that powerful voice we all knew so well, but rattled, so ravaged by cancer. *"Swinger! I'm not dead yet! I'm going to go on the porch and have a picture taken with my grand-daughter!"*

And he did, weak but defiant, Pop emerging onto the porch to have the picture taken. He gave Danie a huge hug and told her how lovely she looked. Afterward, Danie introduced Pop to her friend Marc. Looking at him, inspecting and seemingly approving, Pop then said in that threatening tone, *"Swinger, you take good care of my granddaughter..."*

That was the last time that Pop came out of the house. He passed away ten days later, just where he wanted to be, in his home with his wife at his side.

* * *

This morning I went down to Pam's mother's house to trim the thorn bushes in front of her porch. She wasn't outside, so I went inside to let her know that I was there to do the work and ask her how she liked them trimmed. Seeing her inside, I then asked why she was sitting in the house on such a beautiful, breezy day. She couldn't give me a real reason...

When Pop was still alive, they were always on the porch, enjoying the outside. They would sit there in their designated chairs: Pop reading a book and she just looking out at the cars passing by.

Now, more days than not, she probably won't be sitting outside. No matter how nice the weather may be, that porch will remain mostly vacant.

We all do, but today it dawned on me how much she misses Pop.

* * *

Danie's high school graduation party.

We held it in July to avoid the congestion of the many other grads having their parties the same night or weekend just after the graduation formalities. Another reason for – and benefit of – holding the party in July was the ability to contract with a caterer for the food and a rental company for the chairs, tent and lights. Both are very much in demand early on in the summer.

Yet another reason to hold Danie's party later is the weather here in June. You can never count on it. The saying in Buffalo is: *"If you don't like the weather, just wait ten minutes and it will change."*

We have a garage where the food tables will be setup, a deck and a front porch where the partygoers can go to sit, eat and relax, should the weather turn ugly. Today won't be the normal family cookout crowd. There will be 84 of us.

The chairs, tent and tables arrived on Friday morning: ample time to setup for Saturday's festivities. The lawn was cut and trimmed; Pam's flowers looked great in the garden; the beer was ordered and iced; everything had fallen into place rather nicely. Now all that we needed was the cooperation of the weather. It wasn't to be...

The weathermen had been forecasting rain. So, as Danie and I setup the tables and chairs in the tent and decorated to the graduation-theme, the clouds rolled-in. About half an hour into our job, Danie left the tent, looked-up, then returned quickly to ask whether or not I thought it would rain. Looking outside, I became distraught. The sky was filling with masses of dark rain clouds. Carefully, I told her that, even if it did rain, we have this huge tent with side curtains to keep us dry. Then Pam came out to check on our progress and, as we talked, she motioned to the sky. It had turned even darker. Danie posed the same question to Pam. Pam replied in much the same way as I had.

Well, even before the first guests started to arrive, the skies opened. It not only poured downward, but sideways. It rained all day. So as not to get the guests soaking wet, Pam and I became the official "runners" between the tent and the garage: for beer, second helpings, anything anyone needed. The only thing we couldn't do was use the bathrooms for them...

Sprinting back and forth, serving our guests, Pam and I carved a muddy swath between the tent and garage.

"Hey! This is like Woodstock with roast beef, chicken and pasta!" someone shouted.

"Yea! But they had drugs to ease the pain of the rain..." another added.

Based on the amount of beer and food consumed, a fine time was had by all, regardless of the foul weather. The rain all but stopped by about 8:00 p.m., and Danie's friends and classmates started showing up at about 9:00 p.m. Stopping to say *"Hi!"* to Pam and me and Miko, they then continued-on to the tent and garage, congregating together wherever dry ground was available. We joined them, and while talking with a couple of the boys about their post-graduation plans, one of Danie's friends asked me about going onto the porch and relaxing on the swing and rockers.

"Okay." had barely escaped my mouth when the party moved en masse; chairs from the tent being carried, fellow graduates migrating to the porch.

I stayed up watching TV in the living room long after Pam went to bed. I guess partly to enjoy the fact that our porch was overflowing with friends of Danie, but also to keep a parental eye and ear on the pulse of the partygoers. I wanted them to enjoy their time together, but I didn't want any alcohol involved. At 2:15 a.m., I went out onto the porch and asked them if they could keep the noise down just a little bit. It didn't bother me and I'm sure it didn't keep Pam awake, but I wanted to be courteous to the neighbors.

Simultaneously, they all apologized, saying that they were only talking and didn't mean to be so loud. Danie got a bit defensive, *"Papa, I want to enjoy my friends... I probably won't see them for awhile after tonight!"*

I knew then that, even if they got loud again, I wouldn't ask anyone to leave. I knew too well – just as Danie seemed to sense – that we might never see some of these kids on this porch again. Life does strange things to friendships and relationships.

* * *

Today we were having a garage sale at Mom and Dad's house. I got tired of sitting in the back yard breathing the secondary smoke from Dad's cigarettes so I decided to sit on the front porch and watch for customers.

Mom and Dad are moving into a senior citizens apartment and selling off a lot of junk they have accumulated over 47 years on Sheffield Avenue. While sitting here, I look at my daughter's bike for sale in the driveway and think back to the thousands of times my bike, and my brother's bike, sat in the same spot when we were growing up in this house. I flash back to some of the great times that we had growing up on Sheffield Avenue.

I look out at the street and recall some of the touch football games we played there, not only in the summer, late into the dark of the night when we couldn't even see the ball anymore, but in the winter too, slipping and sliding on the snow and slush. I think back to the hockey games, curb-ball games, and how we "owned" the street when we were young. This street was our playground, our universe.

I look to the spot in the street where big Jim and little Jim Mahoney would play catch with the baseball, and how they would frown at the drivers who dared interrupt their game. I can see Ray and Whitey Miller doing the same; they were college kids who lived next door to the Mahoneys. They threw fastballs that seemed to smoke. They used to put a rubber home plate in the street in order to judge the accuracy of their pitching. I still can hear the popping sound that the ball made as it hit the well-worn pockets of their gloves.

I remember how hard it was for me to leave this house and my family, when I took my first teaching job out of state. I felt a sense of belonging, though, because Mom and Dad still lived here and I was always welcome to come and stay whenever I wanted. My daughters only remember Grandma and Grandpa living in this house.

I can only imagine how my parents might feel the day they back the car out of this driveway for the last time and head up to the end of the street. Looking longingly at each of their neighbors' houses as they pass them by, on their way to another residence. An apartment complex of corridors, concrete and blacktop, their new residence, a senior citizens complex, will be a big change from this place, full of trees, lawns and fine old homes.

I'm glad I'll be at work the day my parents leave Sheffield Avenue.

* * *

It's about 6:30 a.m., another beautiful day of summer and I wave to Pam as I watch her back out of the driveway to go up the street to go to work. She works so close to home that the spark plugs don't even get warm before she gets there and parks.

The cardinals are singing on this beautiful morning. We don't get many songbirds around here; their call is so pretty. We used to have five or six cardinals around here a few summers ago. but now it seems like there are only two or three left. It is so still this morning that I can hear them from the front porch, even though they are in the backyard.

I used to sit with Pop on his porch. Summertime, talking, drinking beer from jelly glasses, and all of a sudden, he would whisper for me to be quiet. Then he'd bring my attention to the nests on the side of Jack's house next door. The birds always built nests in the ivy climbing between the mortar joints and bricks. Pop would say, *"Listen Swinger, the moms and babies are scared. There must be a blue jay nearby."*

Sure as heck, in a few minutes time, the noise from the birds increased, growing louder.

Next thing we saw was a blue jay sweeping into the vines, helping himself to the baby birds while the mom stood by helplessly, screaming. After a few moments, the noise quieted, surrendering to near silence.

To me this seemed so cruel. I guess it was just nature playing itself out like it does everyday out of the sight and hearing of humans. That day though, we witnessed it, and today, years later, I still think about it. I can hear the sounds and silence of those birds in my mind.

It is surely a strange phenomenon, when the beautiful singing of a cardinal can trigger thoughts of birds being preyed upon, screaming for their lives.

* * *

While going to visit my sister Janie today, I drove by Mom and Dad's house on Sheffield Avenue. I slowed down when I saw the "For Sale" sign on the front lawn. It was the first time that I had seen it since Mom and Dad listed the house for sale after moving into their senior citizens complex. I have a thousand memories of that front lawn in the forty-seven years that we lived there. For a second I flashed back to a couple in particular.

One was when Dad, our neighbor from across the street Kenny, Uncle Tommy and Grandpa Gugliotti were digging up the lawn to put in either a sewer or water line. I was real little at the time and can't remember which. Uncle Tommy brought a cute little puppy with him and that puppy was playing in the grass. All of a sudden, the puppy started to chase me, wanting to play with me. I got scared, ran around like crazy and nearly fell into the hole. They all laughed so hard at me for being afraid of a puppy.

The other was when Aunt Nicky wrestled cousin Frankie on the porch. The wrestling match spilled onto the driveway, where she proceeded to give him the sleeper hold. She was real upset with him and let him have it real good. He was begging for her to stop. I had never heard of nor seen Frankie back away from a fight or any confrontation, but that day, he had his hands full.

That "For Sale" sign made me ponder, struggle with, finality. I knew that I would no longer be able to walk on that lawn or jump over those shrubs that Dad had fussed over for so many years. I would not put my feet up on that porch railing ever again.

When that "For Sale" sign becomes a "Sold" sign, my physical ties to 193 Sheffield Avenue will be broken. But my mental ties will only be as far away as my mind.

Author's current home at 53 Erie Street: post-rehab, children, and a lifetime of experiences (so far...).

Pam is sitting on the porch reading one of those fat books that seem to take her months to finish. We just ate dinner and Miko took off somewhere with her boyfriend. We are alone.

Pam is listening to this tiny transistor radio that is made to look like a boom box. We received it in a *"get a quote from us"* insurance promotion. She has the volume down low and, for some reason, it reminds me of the transistor radios that her and I and thousands of other Baby Boomers had when we were in our late elementary school and high school years. There were no such things as boom boxes, ghetto blasters, walkmans, portable CD players, or iPods back then. Our songs came from little leather- or vinyl-clad radios powered by transistors and 9-volt batteries.

Not too long ago, Danie saw one of Pam's old transistor radios in the cabinet, picked it up and asked what it was. When we told her, she declared, *"No way this thing plays music!"* So I popped a 9-volt battery into it, powered it up, and Danie roared in delight when she heard the music.

I still remember what I received as an 8th grade graduation gift from Holy Family Grade School in South Buffalo. It was a sixteen-transistor model, double the power of the eight-transistor radio that I used to have. I remember that graduation night, listening to music through the flesh-colored earphone. I thought it was the greatest present ever.

Funny how the most advanced technology is now a relic to my daughter. She even laughed at it. How rude!

* * *

Everyone says it's hard to see your first one go off to college, especially if they are relocating to another city or town. Danie will be attending Temple University in Philadelphia, putting us out of easy driving range, making this more difficult on all of us: fewer weekend visits; the only benefit being fewer bags of dirty laundry. Like all parents, I love my girls to the "upteenth degree." Or, as I always tell them, *"I love you tons and bunches."* I will have a hard time dealing with Danie's departure and distance.

As I look at the van, packed to the roof, I am at least grateful that we are almost out of things to put in it. The thermos bottle of coffee for Pam and me, AAA maps, Miko's pillow for napping there and back... Barely awake, Miko comes through the door and onto the porch, looking like there are a million places she'd rather be. Pam locks the back door and walks up the driveway.

At last, Danie comes outside. In one hand is her security bunny as old as she is, and a backpack is slung over her other shoulder. I whisper to her to make sure the front door is locked, and she does so, turns, then heads towards me, at the base of the porch steps. She stops.

"Hold on a second." Looking at me, she asks, *"Why Papa?"*

And I can see her walking off the porch on her way to kindergarten, also with a backpack over her shoulder. Now she is off to college. Where does time go?

"Papa, don't worry about me," Danie says, *"I'll be fine."*

"It's not you I'm worried about..."

Smiling, she then tenders, *"We should go now."*

So we did.

* * *

The day of Miko's Senior Prom has arrived. She will have spent most of the day getting her hair done just right, showering what seemed like five times, doing her makeup, and applying all of the accoutrements that will make her beautiful. Before the day is done, she will have called upon Pam probably a hundred times to check on something or another; things that only moms and daughters understand.

Today is also the day that our high school's male faculty members have our "almost-the end-of-the-year party." There is always lots of food, beverages of all sorts, cigars, a bonfire that can be seen for miles, and an abundance of verbal jousting that a person with an easily bruised ego might find injurious to their mental health and well being. In all, there is camaraderie, male bonding, and a release of energy that makes the last few weeks of the school year seem more tolerable.

Last year, there was a conflict with me attending the party versus seeing my daughter all dressed-up for her Junior Prom. To the chagrin of Pam, I chose male camaraderie over seeing Miko off. The decision was not as easy as it might seem, but I knew that Pam would take wonderful pictures. She did and Miko looked beautiful.

This year will be different, though. Not only because it's her Senior Prom, but because we were clandestinely notified that Miko and her boyfriend were going to be crowned Prom Queen and King. I knew then that no amount of justification would do this time. The faculty party would have to take a backseat. As if I needed the prodding, Pam told me that if I was not home for the viewing and didn't attend the Prom festivities this time, this year, I would, *"Not have a home to come home to..."*

A handful of the guys gave me static about my priorities, but the rest were supportive of Pam's insistence. Predictably, one told me to go to the party and sleep out under the stars, since that would be my home from now on. A short-term solution if ever there was one!

After making sure that my burnable contribution to the bonfire was going to be transported by another teacher, I drove home from school, pouting. Arriving and parking, I was pretty much ignored, and when I was noticed, I was in the way and told to get out of the way. I was soon relegated to being the "fetch it guy." You would almost think this was Miko's wedding instead of her Prom...

Eventually, after what seemed like hours, Pam told me to get the camera and meet them on the porch for the pre-Prom pictures of Miko. This was a custom in our house – to take pictures of the girls on the porch – anytime they were dressed up for any special event. We did it with Danie, and now, Miko. These porch pictures could fill up an album all by themselves: whether of the girls, family members or get-togethers, I've done this countless times, and thought this photo session would be like all the rest. I was sorely mistaken...

I grabbed the camera and focused for Miko to step outside onto the porch. Pam opened the door, and the girl I was so used to seeing in tomboy or athletic attire, now emerged as a lovely young lady. My eyes traveled from her head to her feet two or three times before I gasped *"Miko..."*

"Papa?" Looking down at her feet, spreading her dress out, lifting her head and looking back at me, Miko asked, *"Papa, do you think I'm beautiful?"*

Trying to clear the lump in my throat, I managed to say, *"No... I think you are more than beautiful."*

"I knew he would think so." chimed-in Pam, and I tried to capture this beauty in digital high resolution. I didn't want to lose this image; my baby girl was now a woman.

Successful, they both disappeared back into the house to gather all Miko would need on this most special night. I remained on the porch, waiting until they came out. It was time for us to leave; the Prom Queen was on her way.

Walking past, Pam said in a low voice, *"Now, you tell me... What was more important tonight?"*

* * *

Miko's boyfriend and I were sitting on the porch steps as she readied herself for their date. We talked about their volleyball game the night before; they both play on the same team in a bar league. I questioned him as to where they were going on their date, then gave him my standard speech. *"Drive carefully, don't stay out too late and don't do dumb things..."*

As we sat there, a van drove by and tooted the horn – a friend of mine and his wife – and I waved as they passed. A short time later, a car went by and gave two long blasts of the horn. I waved again.

Intrigued, Miko's boyfriend said, *"Gee, you know everybody!"*

Grinning, I admitted that I had no clue who was in that last car. Perplexed, he wondered why I waved if I didn't know them?

I wave to anyone who beeps at me while I'm on the porch or in the front yard, I said. Whether or not I immediately recognize them, I wouldn't want to offend anyone passing by, offering a kind beep.

They obviously know me – That's all that matters – And a wave is certainly in order.

* * *

Yesterday we had one of our typical summer down-pours. There was thunder and a bit of lighting up north but all we caught was the heavy rain. I was watching television inside and, in addition to the rain pounding on the roof, lawn and driveway, I could hear another sound. Curious, I went to the front door, only to be rewarded with a waterfall of rain, overflowing from the gutter and falling onto the porch floor.

Not knowing how long it would rain, I decided to not take any chances with the porch floor becoming satu-rated, and went into Danie's bedroom and climbed out onto the porch roof in the midst of the downpour. Almost im-mediately, I found the cause of the overflowing gutter: leaves had accumulated in the downspout diverter. I cleaned them out and watched the water flow downward, properly, away from the porch. Still, I knew I'd be back up tomorrow – today – finishing the job, doing it right, and hopefully without getting soaked through.

Today, using a bit more common sense in my ap-proach, I used the extension ladder. I proceeded with my gutter-cleaning routine and was surprised at what I found in the gutter on the north side of the porch. Over an area of about six linear feet, there was $0.67 in change inside the gutter. Not knowing how all those dimes, nickels and pen-nies got there, I put them in my pocket, then finished the task and put the ladder back in the garage.

The coins were closest to Danie's bedroom window so I started my investigation with her. I had no idea how she would explain those coins in the gutter, but she did. It seems, one night a week or so ago, Marc, her good friend from high school, came to visit at 2:00 a.m. Not wanting to wake the rest of the family with a phone call or ringing the doorbell, Marc pelted Danie's bedroom window with coins. The coins obviously bounced off of the window or house siding then wound up in the gutter, but they still did the trick: Danie woke-up and went downstairs to greet him. They sat on the porch and talked for hours.

The next time Marc came by, I questioned his tactics. Understandably, he thought that I was upset about the late night visit. I wasn't at all, more confused, and only asked why he threw the coins. He answered that he couldn't find any stones to throw.

After explaining to him that I was only concerned about a window breaking, Marc assured me that he threw them softly. Danie sleeps like a corpse, so it had to be more than soft...

Wanting to show him that I was truly not upset, I decided that a bit of levity might work.

"Marc, is that all you think my daughter is worth, sixty-seven cents?"

Blushing, he was forced to admit, "A*ctually, I didn't even want to spend that much. But I had a hard time waking her up!*"

* * *

Danie is home from college for the Christmas holidays. As is usual in Western New York, you never know when Mother Nature will deal a cruel blow. We awoke this morning to about nineteen inches of snow.

Before coming home, Danie called us from her dorm to tell us that Philadelphia was bracing itself for a snowstorm. Afterward, she called and said that the snow had come, reaching the laughable depth of four inches: a "dusting" by our standards. But Philadelphia was practically shutdown; even Temple University was closed for a few days.

Home now, and nineteen inches later, I was outside clearing the snow, finishing sweeping-off the porch floor with a broom. And Danie came out onto the porch in shorts, flip-flops and a t-shirt to say good morning. She often brags how she walks around in a sweatshirt when winter hits Philadelphia, and today was no different. Buffalo thickens the skin, even when students from other climates think a natural disaster has occurred, and here she was, asking if I was almost done.

She wanted to go get some post-Christmas bargains at the mall, and I told her I would ready in a few minutes. Heading back into the house, Danie turned, held up both arms, then declared, *"Papa, now this is what I call a dusting!"*

* * *

As I pull into the driveway, home from school, the huge icicles hanging from the house roof and over the porch roof catch my eye. Because of the age of our house, dating back to at least 1847, plank and beam construction was used. This means that there are no areas in the walls to run heat ducts. A furnace in the basement heats the first floor of the house. The second floor is heated by furnace that is housed in the area that many would call an attic; in our house it is just the area above the ceiling, too small to be considered an attic.

Because of the heat generated by the upper furnace in the winter, snow melts off the roof shingles and drips down toward the outer edges. There it accumulates and compounds into a waterfall of ice usually ten inches thick and fifteen feet long, covering the porch roof and hanging usually four feet below. Cascading downward, the ice builds a dam along the porch roof that can grow to almost a foot thick. I never put gutters on this portion of the roof, knowing that this annual icing will bulge and inevitably rip them right off the house.

After seeing another annual waterfall of ice, I go into the house and tell Pam that I have to deal with it once more. This is a regular event, and Pam responds as usual, *"Be careful."*

"If I fall and die, you get the Corvette. Just don't use it as a man magnet until I'm cold in the ground." I say (only half in jest), then gather my tools of battle: hammer, chisel, pickaxe, ladder and safety glasses.

Positioning the ladder, I slowly ascend until I am ready to step atop the porch roof. Leaning and planting my feet, I have a hard time getting a grip in the snow; it covers that sheet of ice and finding good footing up here is a delicate task. I feel like Tenzing Norgay, looking at the great Ice Fall of Mount Everest, but comforted by the thought that if I do fall, it will only be thirteen feet or so to the ground, not thousands.

Slow and steady, every step careful, I make my way to the icicles hanging from the edge of the overhead roof. Putting on the safety glasses, I stretch to pound the hammer into the face of the ice, hoping to get lucky and only have to use one tool instead of many. I hear that dead thud. This is a thick sheet indeed; the chisel will be required today.

Over the course of an hour or so, fingers numbing despite insulated gloves, I manage to clear the icicles from the roof edge. They now lay atop the porch roof, around my feet, ready to be hurled to the ground below. Once removed, my next chore is breaking-up the ice dam. A pickaxe is required for this task, but it must be handled with surgical precision. If I don't drive the pickaxe into the ice hard and deep enough, I will be here forever. But, if I drive it into the ice too deeply, it might dig into the asphalt shingles, causing holes and untold damage to the roof.

At last successful - for another year at least - I throw everything off of the porch roof - miscellaneous tools, chunks of ice - down to the ground below. This too must be handled with care because, just below the overhang of the roof, is Pam's flower garden. She tends it with great care and, in years past, I have injured the Japanese dwarf red maple and disfigured many of her plants into unrecognizable mounds – only to be discovered after spring thaw.

Now I can make my way down the ladder. Strangely, the descent seems to be three feet shorter, with all of that ice from the roof now covering the ground. The job has taken me nearly two hours today: a little longer than usual because the ice was so thick. Feet firmly planted, I look up to the sky, nod and smile, thankful for allowing me to finish the job without slipping or falling.

Hands by now frozen through, lifeless, almost useless, I put all of the tools and the ladder away, then wander back to look at my accomplishment. Standing there staring, feeling satisfied, for a second I think ahead to the time when we will sell this house. I wonder if the new owner will deal with the ice situation in the same way? Then I wonder: If we wind up selling the house in the winter, and all that ice is hanging there, will it turn prospective buyers off? Or will they find it charming, another element, a reason to buy a house over 150 years old? This annual task is as necessary as any other on this wonderful house; will I dare tell them all that goes into clearing the ice and dam? Will they be turned off?

Will I? Will they?

* * *

Today, August 14, 2003, Pam and I brought Miko and her possessions back to college. She is now a sophomore at Niagara University, just outside of Niagara Falls. She is on a scholarship with the volleyball team. From that first day holding her on the porch as a baby, I knew she was going to be an athlete! But, as an athlete participating in a fall sport, she has to be back at school by mid-August for training and practice. This means that she gets to move into the dorms early and avoid the crunch when all the other students return a few weeks later.

Since we performed this routine last year, we knew what to expect and the entire process went pretty smoothly. Just as we were about to leave there was a power blackout for a few seconds, but the juice was restored quickly and we dismissed it without much thought. We hugged and kissed her goodbye, then drove off campus and back to the highway, leaving our adult daughter behind for another semester.

Listening to the radio on the way back home, it became more apparent that that brief blackout wasn't so brief after all, and a few minutes later the radio described the problem as impacting more than just the Niagara Falls area. Listening for the updates felt like waiting for the school closing reports when it snows.

"I wonder who's next?" we wondered aloud. When we heard *"Lancaster"* Pam and I looked at each other. *"Uh-ohhh..."*

Before we got off of the highway, we called Danie on the cell phone and asked if she wanted some food. Without power, we will be having an unconventional dinner. I was thinking about hot dogs on the grill, but we decided to stop at a restaurant along the way. They were all without power, too – fast food needs fast customers – so we bought what was available and went home. There, we got the candles and flashlights out of storage and then ate our ad hoc supper. Since there was no electric for lights or any of the other conveniences we have come to know and enjoy in our lifetime, we relocated to the porch. Pam, Danie and I were not alone; our neighbors decided to head for their porches, too.

Each house along our street glowed of candles and the occasional flicker of a flashlight, front porches full of people sitting, talking in hushed tones. The darkness seemed to have inspired silence; a nervous yet comforting quiet. Even the cars venturing down the street seemed to be going slower, their motors rumbling low.

We soon received news over Pam's transistor radio that the power outage wasn't just local, but had in fact spread across the northeast and into Canada. The announcer said that the cause of the blackout was not known and might not be known for many hours more.

Pam and I actually enjoyed the peacefulness, the novelty of quiet darkness. Danie, on the other hand, a soon-to-be college senior, was becoming a basket case. She was getting antsy, repeatedly asking, *"When will it end?"*

She wondered if this is what it was like before electricity. I assured her that it was. She asked what she was supposed to do if she had to go to the bathroom? I told her to take a candle. *"Oh God!"*

Then she asked if the toilet would even flush without electricity? I told that water and gravity need no electricity. Becoming more agitated as the time passed, no end to the darkness in sight, Danie huffed, *"That's it! I'm going inside and getting online. I'm bored out of my mind out here! I've had enough peace and quiet to last me a lifetime!"*

Laughing, I informed her that even AOL needs power.

As she walked into the house in disgust, mumbling something about the whereabouts of the cell phone, Danie said to no one in particular, *"I never could've been born in the good old days, this really sucks..."*

* * *

My mom is sitting on the porch with Pam and me. We decided that a few days away from my father would be good for them both. Mom has Alzheimer's.

She was diagnosed with symptoms of the disease just a couple of years ago. It has progressed to the point where she repeats herself and asks the same questions over and over. Her driving privileges were taken away at the recommendation of her neurologist, and Mom and Dad are now being assisted by their children.

Dad can't keep giving her the care that she needs any longer so we have started the search for an adult care facility for her. We know that she will not want to be in an adult care facility. We have been told that others cry and plead to go back home. However cold, we have also been told to hope the memory loss is rapid, so she loses touch, becomes resigned. I find this hard to swallow, but I'm readying myself for anything. Whatever happens, it won't be easy.

The interim solution is to help Dad by giving him some quality time for himself. At the same time, Mom gets a break too, seeing other people, spending time with us on our porch.

Pam is great with her. She treats Mom like she used to treat Danie and Miko when they were younger. She knows how to reason with her, never lose her temper. She even got Mom to eat eggs for breakfast – a food that Mom doesn't even like – using sweet and juicy slices of cantaloupe as encouragement to clear her plate.

Today, looking at Mom, sitting on the porch, I tell myself that this could very well be the last time that she sits in one of these rockers. Witnessing her struggle with here and now, a lifetime of memories...

She talks in circles, and we all try to listen. We told the girls that, when Grandma asks the same question over again, they are to answer it like they just heard it for the first time. Both have become accustomed to it.

Sitting here, thinking, listening to Mom talk about old friends, distant places, a train passes by. The tracks run along the rear of our property and we get four or five freight trains each day. We almost don't hear them anymore.

"There goes a train."

Mom said that; she stopped in mid-sentence to say, *"There goes a train."*

And I pause to look at her. She is back, my mother, like before this dreaded disease overtook her. And us...

And she starts to talk about when she was a young girl, and would visit Aunt Nellie's near Lackawanna. She says the trains running alongside the house used to scare all of the chickens out of the coop. Describes Aunt Nellie running around, shooing them back into that coop, flapping her apron, scaring those chickens even worse.

Mom seems to remember it so clearly, vividly, like it happened only yesterday. And I swear she's giggling as she shares that story.

Then, in a matter of only minutes, she is gone again. Staring off, asking the same questions.

Pam and Mom are soon engaged in another one-sided conversation, and I glance up the sidewalk to our old, aged neighbor's house. His wife had Alzheimer's. A few years ago, visiting him after she went into a nursing home, I followed that same sidewalk home. I remember asking God to never let this disease strike anyone near and dear to me.

I guess He didn't hear me.

* * *

It's the first weekend in September, marking the beginning of the last year of college for Danie at Temple University. She was home in Lancaster for the summer but now, reluctantly, it was time that we drove her back to Philadelphia to help her clean her portion of the apartment she has shared for the past school year with a bunch of her teammates from the volleyball team.

For her senior year, Danie would be moving from this old, red brick, three-floor row house, located in what she and her roommates lovingly referred to as "*the ghetto*." They will be moving into a warehouse that was just recently converted into loft apartments. Philadelphia is a forward-looking city when it comes to housing needs for college students. Although the move was just to the other side of campus, but actually still off-campus, it was a move that would physically offer somewhat more safety and security. Her new building had a manned security desk and residents have to swipe ID cards in order to gain access to the non-common areas, elevators and apartments. Pam and I greeted this move with much anticipation and parental relief.

Danie always spoke about the people that lived on the block that she was moving from as "*people who watched out for us*." To some this might seem strange, but Danie, her roommates, and a house up the block – also full of Temple University students on the baseball team – were the only white residents on the entire block. Danie and her roommates had earned the privilege of being watched-out for by watching-out for and caring for the little kids on the block. They gave the kids jigsaw puzzles, read books to them, took them to parks to play, tossed footballs and Frisbees with them, and even gave them little Christmas gifts. Pam and I always supported our daughter and her friends in doing this, and felt good that they were giving their little buddies both emotional and physical gifts.

Having been born on the East Side of Buffalo - an area made up of Italians, African Americans and Puerto Ricans – racial diversity is nothing new to me. For years, my Uncle John and Dad owned and operated our Italian importing grocery store in that same locale. Back then, the residents referred to the area as *"the neighborhood."* To-day, it, and seemingly all of the adjoining areas, have taken-on the title of being just *"the hood."* The East Side of Buffalo is now replete with the problems of many inner city areas: drugs, gangs and the violence that always seem to follow.

After cleaning Danie's room and assembling her possessions for the movers, we got to spend some time on her apartment porch. In this case, the word *"porch"* is a misnomer because it was actually just a four- by four-foot square, four-inch thick concrete slab with concrete steps. There is not a single piece of wood in the structure. I would call it a stoop. Behind us was the exterior door cov-ered with iron security bars.

Pam and Danie and I sat and made small talk and, after a while, a little girl came running up and shouted, *"Miss Danie!"* and gave my daughter a big hug. *"I missed you so much!"*

A short time later, two little boys came by and shouted to Danie. Danie left the stoop to hug them and talk about how their summer was going. Not long after that, the lady next door came out to see what all the yelling was about. She greeted Danie in a loud voice, then Danie introduced us and we all had a short but pleasant conversation. The lady was disappointed to learn that the volleyball girls were moving away, and Danie told her and the kids that she would also miss them.

Throughout, I peered from my perch on the stoop, soaking up the sights and sounds of the block my daughter had called home for the past year. It was a different version of "*the neighborhood.*" These stoops weren't wooden like where I grew-up, and each had wrought iron railings. Many had no roofs overhead, as most had given way to dry rot and decay long ago. There was barely room enough for four people to stand elbow-to-elbow, let alone an entire family trying to out-shout each other for conversation rights, as was often the case in my neighborhood and, it seems, here too. Even so, these stoops had two or three aluminum, vinyl-webbed lawn chairs on them; not exactly giving the look or sense of "*welcome to my home*" that I had become accustomed to while growing-up or today in Lancaster. To be fair, to the people who gather on these stoops, my porch might be an alien structure as well, as confounding as an igloo to a desert nomad.

What these stoops did have, though, were items usually found on porches in more affluent neighborhoods. There were pretty potted plants, railing planters with hanging flowers, small propane cooking grills, empty beverage containers, and one even had the remnants of Christmas decorations that seemed to be permanently affixed to the railings. These stoops that I had overlooked while driving-up had taken a new identity, another reality, functionality.

Whatever their structural or financial situation, these stoops to these neighbors are what my porch is to me. In fact, they may even represent much more.

Compared to mine, these stoops actually incite conversation; it's easier to hear and reply from a stoop. Here, neighbors can talk without yelling – fewer driveways, smaller lawns, no fences to outdo, only each other.

Here, everyone can be heard.

* * *

My sister asked me if I was interested in rebuilding a porch floor for one of her neighbors. Many years ago, for the previous owner of the house, I had built the porch steps, so I told her that I'd look into it. I met the new owner and he told me that he wanted to tear the old floor up and put down a new one of pressure-treated lumber. I took some measurements and got back to him in a few days with a price. He agreed and I gave him a date when I could do the work.

Being that it was summer and Miko was home from college, I asked her if she was interested in making a few dollars. Of course, she said *"Sure!"*

Miko and I had done many things together but never for pay. This was a whole new experience for both of us, so we tore-up the old pine, spending two days sweating beside each other. Miko asked plenty of questions: about my old remodeling business and the many jobs I did back then, even my ex-partner, who has since passed-on. I still consider him one of my best friends.

Miko marveled at the tricks of the trade, and I showed her how to use a wooden wedge to lay the new boards.

"Do all carpenters know this trick or was it all your idea?" she asked, watching the two boards come together with ease.

"Yes and no," I answered, *"The good carpenters know this trick, so no, it wasn't my original idea."* Sensing opportunity, I then turned this trick on her, saying that she should have learned it in school: simple machines are basic

science and the inclined plane or wedge is one of them. Her science teacher never taught that, she said, probably skipping that lesson because there was no practical application to apply the theory. At last, here was a fine demonstration, hands-on no less, care of Dad and a needy porch.

We finished the job in two days, no problems whatsoever, and the owner was extremely happy with the result. Another porch for another person...

After subtracting our expenses, Miko and I were glad to see we had managed to make a nice profit. But we knew that already, beyond money, we were now closer, richer, than ever.

* * *

While sitting on the porch earlier today, Pam commented how beautiful the weather was.

You couldn't buy a cloud out of the sky if you tried, it was extremely hot, no humidity whatsoever, and the weather report called for the same tomorrow. I agreed with her, but added that it would be a lot more bearable if there was a breeze to help cool things down a little.

Hearing this, Pam looked over at me from her spot on the porch swing, seeming to scowl and smile at the same time, she then spoke the truth:

"Listen Mister! This is what we wait nine months for... Enjoy it! And quiet your whining..."

About the Author

Angelo Daluisio is a Technology Education Teacher at Orchard Park High School, and lives in Lancaster, New York with his wife Pam. They have two daughters, Danielle and Micole, and with the help of family and friends, Angelo and Pam have gutted and rehabbed – at times reincarnated - two homes too many.

Angelo remains active in the local community, coaching and refereeing, and helps friends and neighbors with home repair and construction projects. He also serves as co-adviser for the Yearbook and the Technology Club, teaching both students and adults the nuances of materials, woodworking and craftsmanship.

This book was to be only a diary – a compilation of two decades of memories and experiences – combined, though, *Porch Passages* is powerful.

This is Angelo Daluisio's first published work.

boofalo@aol.com

About the Publisher

Kookalook Publishing was founded in 1997 in Buffalo, New York by Brad Lockwood to produce and promote independent, experimental literary works. In addition to this book, **Rhapsodies & Requiems** – a collection of illustrations and prose by the ever-evolving Jamie Kuntz – was released in 2003 (ISBN # 0-9706323-9-8).

Lockwood's novella **Sellout** (ISBN # 0-9706323-0-4) was published in 2000, and its 2 CD-set audio companion in 2001 (ISBN # 0-9706323-1-2). Nominated for multiple *"Audie Awards"* for both performance and production excellence, **Sellout** has achieved remarkable sales and critical acclaim. Lockwood's latest novel - **Wink** (ISBN # 0-595-65439-8) released in 2003 – is a mysterious and hilarious treatise on high technology.

His forthcoming book – Brad Lockwood's first major non-fiction work - **Tested XX – The Case Cutlery Dynasty** tells the triumphant yet tragic tale of America's oldest and largest family of knife-makers: His own.

Serving many genres – fiction, non-fiction, poetry, and children – as well as mediums – print, audio, video and film – Kookalook Publishing is now based in Brooklyn.

kookypubs@hotmail.com